BIG-NOTE PIANO

The BEST CHRISTMAS MUSIC

T0048405

ISBN 978-0-7935-8436-9

HAL•LEONARD®
CORPORATION
7777 W. BLUEMOUND RD. P.O. BOX 13819 MILWAUKEE, WI 53213

Visit Hal Leonard Online at
www.halleonard.com

ANGELS WE HAVE HEARD ON HIGH

19th Century French Carol

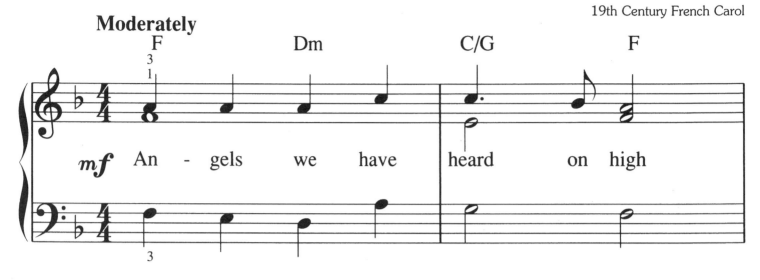

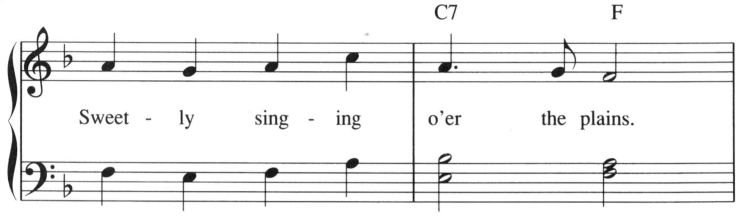

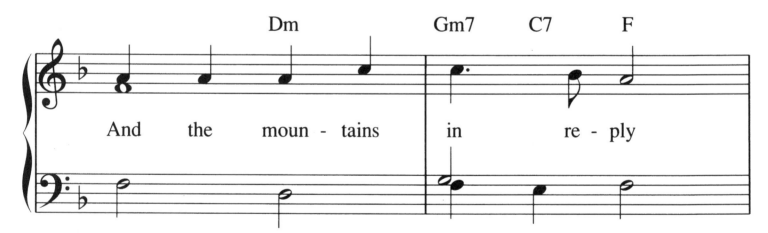

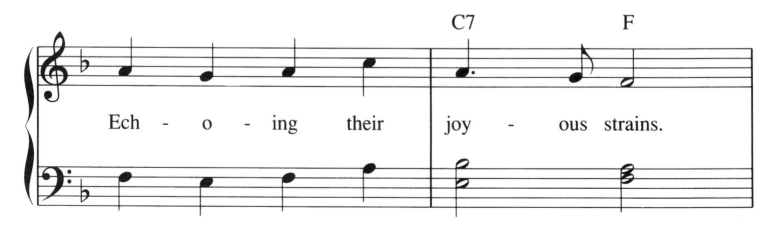

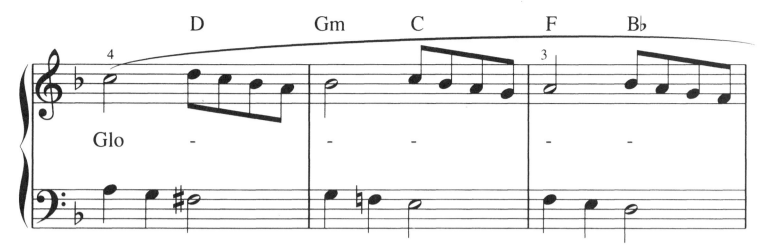

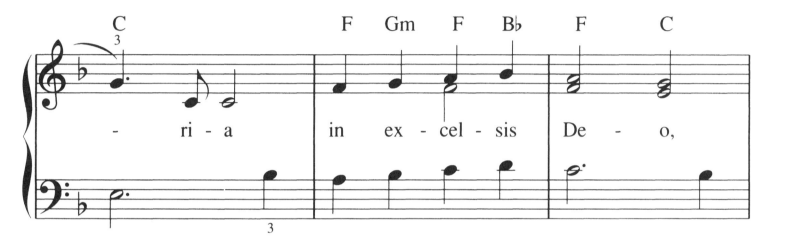

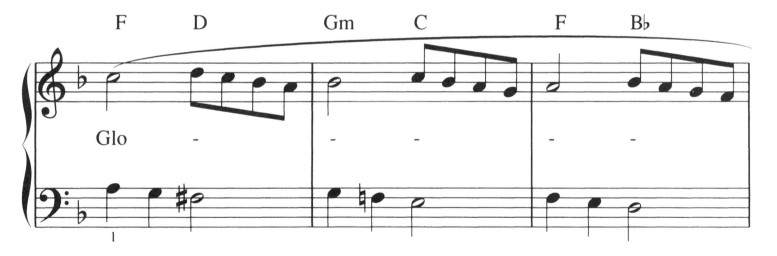

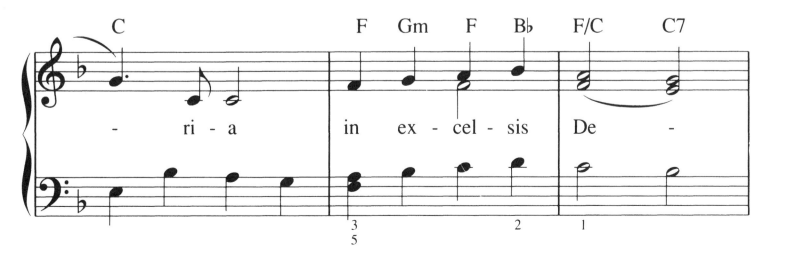

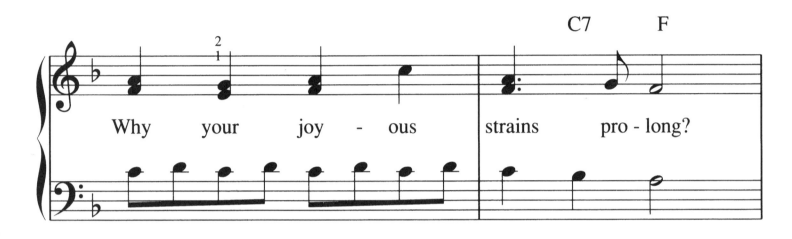

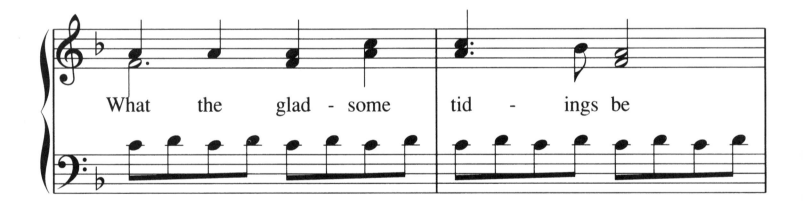

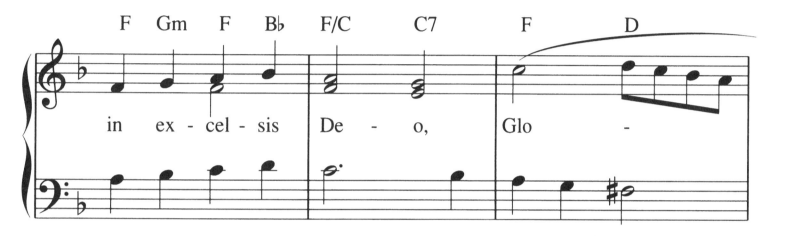

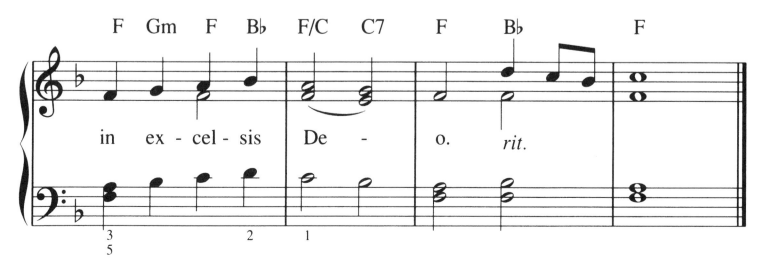

AWAY IN A MANGER

Anonymous Text (vv.1,2)
Text by JOHN T. McFARLAND (v.3)
Music by JONATHAN E. SPILLMAN

Slow Waltz

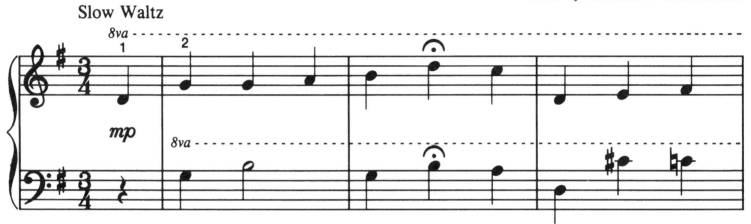

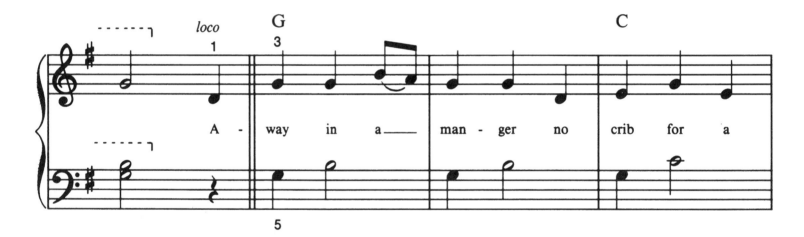

A - way in a manger no crib for a

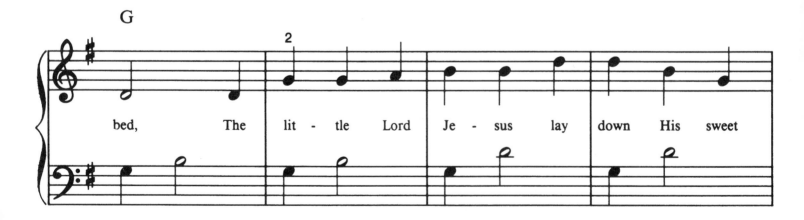

bed, The lit - tle Lord Je - sus lay down His sweet

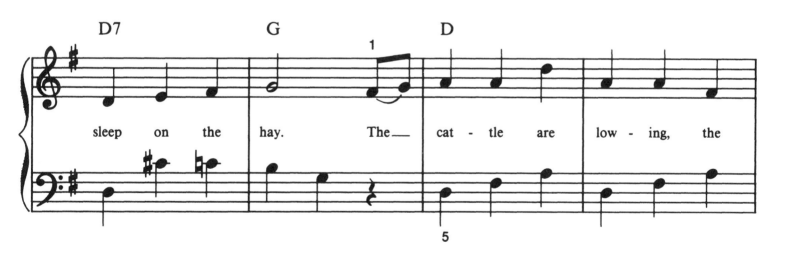

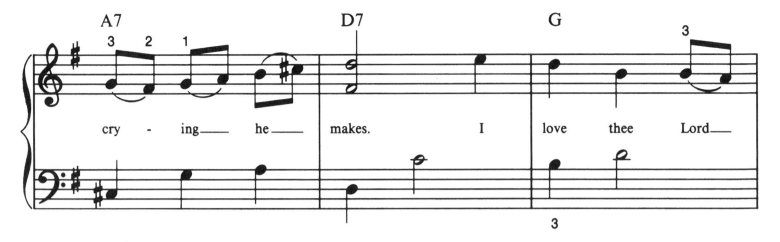

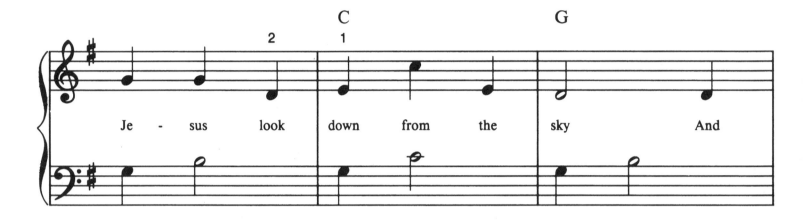

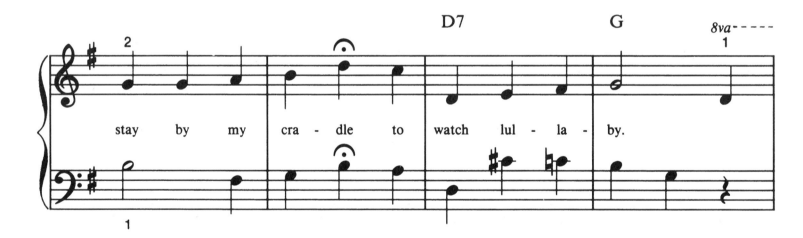

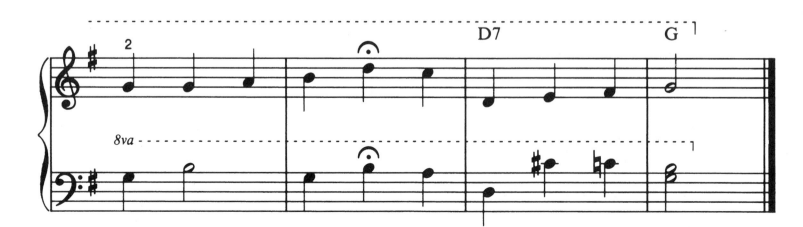

BLUE CHRISTMAS

Words and Music by BILLY HAYES
and JAY JOHNSON

Slowly

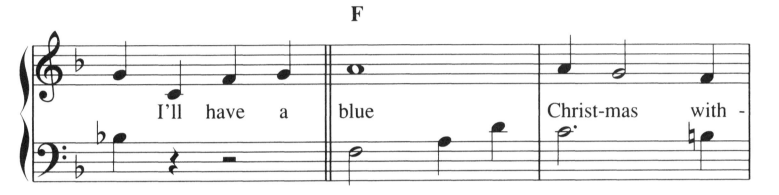

I'll have a blue Christ-mas with-

out you. I'll be so blue

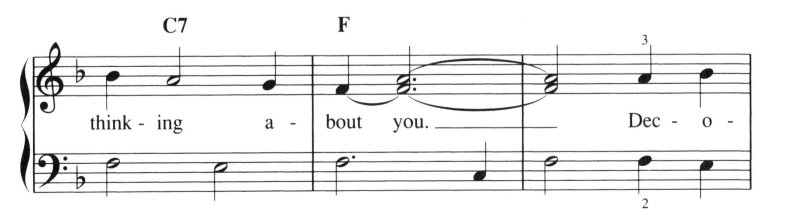

think - ing a - bout you. Dec - o -

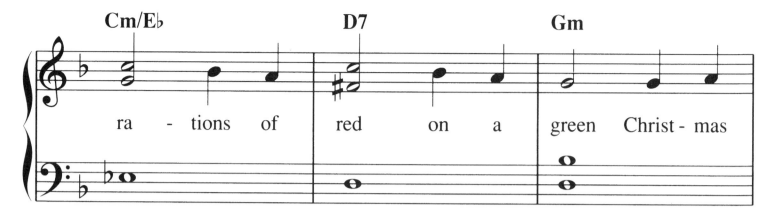

ra - tions of | red on a | green Christ - mas

tree | won't mean a | thing if

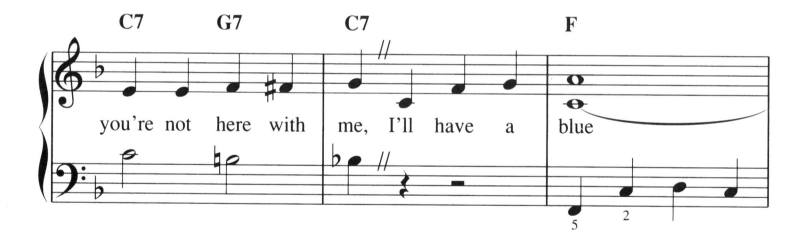

you're not here with | me, I'll have a | blue

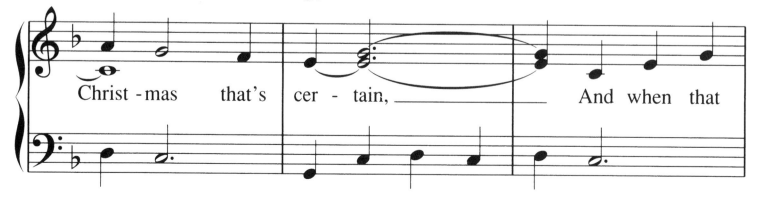

Christ - mas that's | cer - tain, _____ | And when that

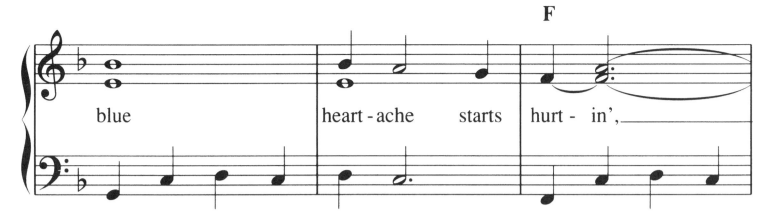

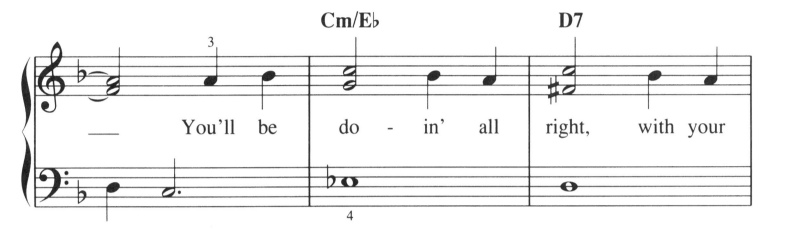

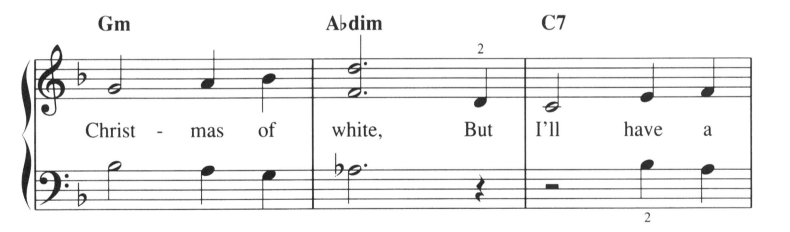

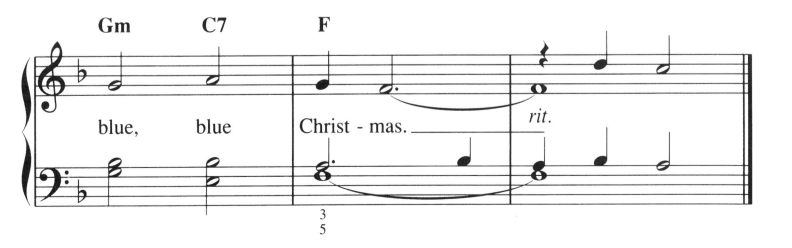

BRING A TORCH, JEANNETTE, ISABELLA

17th Century French Provencal Carol

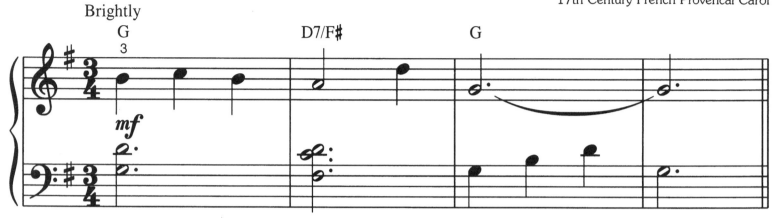

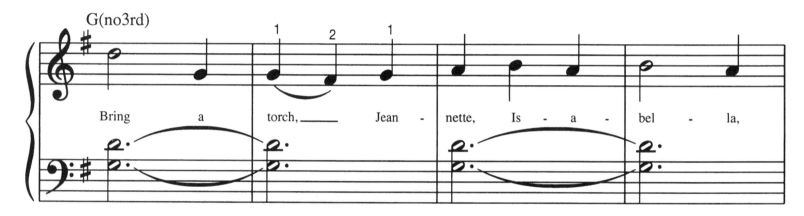

Bring a torch,____ Jean - nette, Is - a - bel - la,

Bring a torch ____ come swift - ly and run.

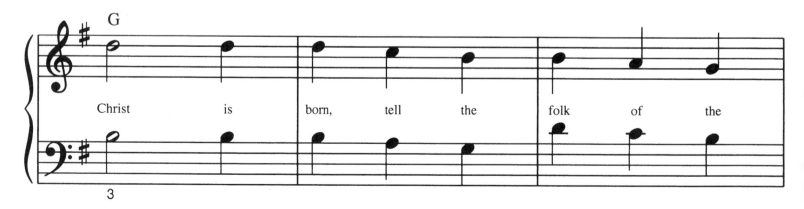

Christ is born, tell the folk of the

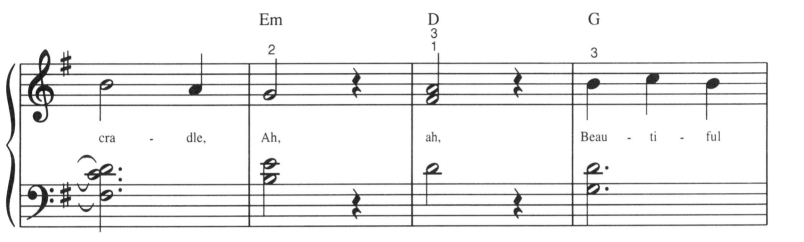

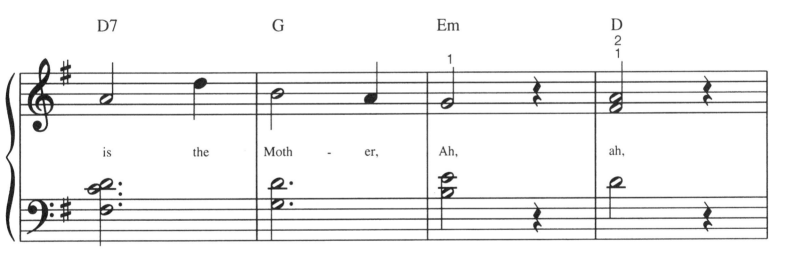

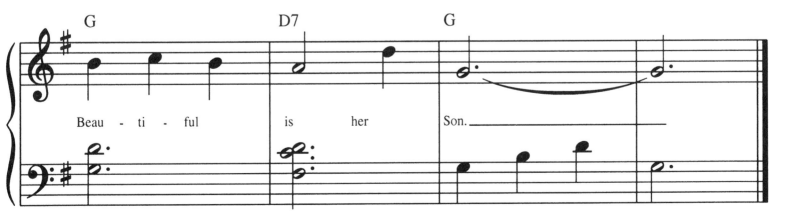

THE CHIPMUNK SONG

Words and Music by
ROSS BAGDASARIAN

Happily

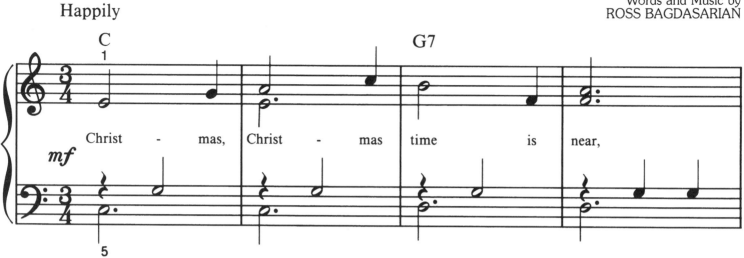

Christ - mas, Christ - mas time is near,

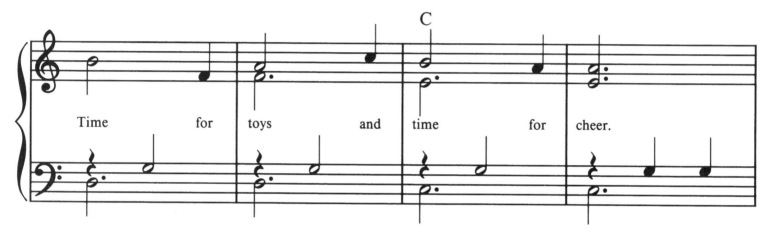

Time for toys and time for cheer.

We've been good but we can't last,

Hur - ry Christ - mas, hur - ry fast!

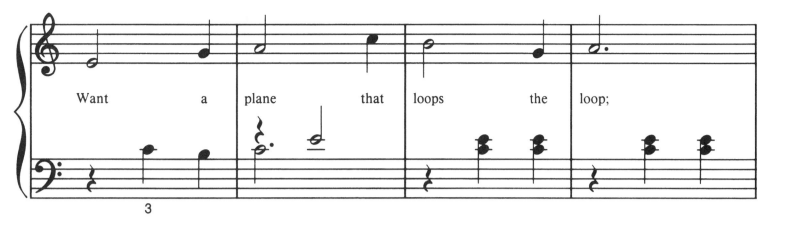

Want a plane that loops the loop;

Me, I want a hu - la hoop.

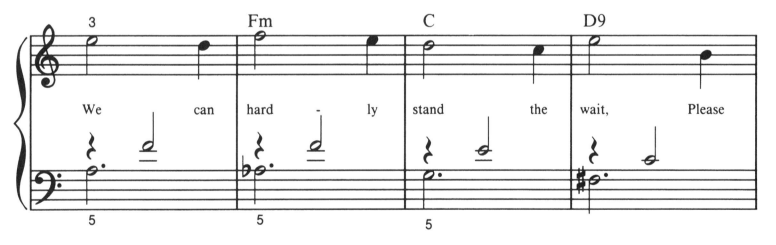

We can hard - ly stand the wait, Please

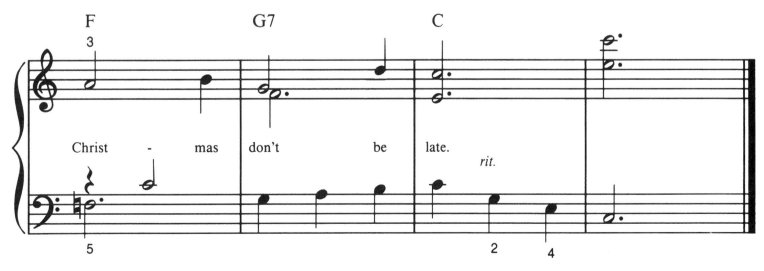

Christ - mas don't be late. *rit.*

C-H-R-I-S-T-M-A-S

Words by JENNY LOU CARSON
Music by EDDY ARNOLD

Moderately

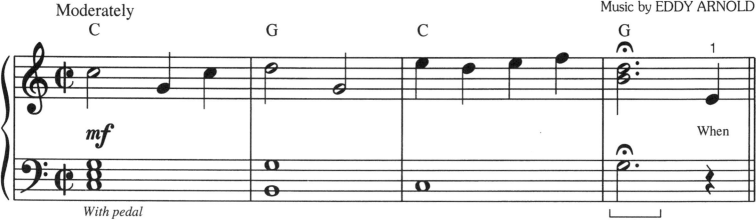

When

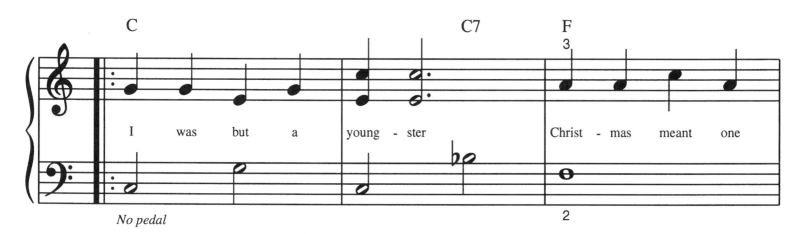

I was but a young-ster   Christ-mas meant one

thing   That   I'd   be   get - ting   lots   of   toys   that

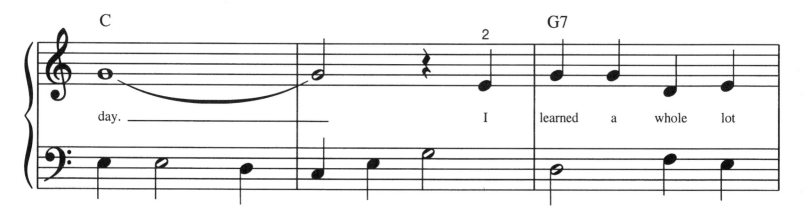

day. _____   I   learned   a   whole   lot

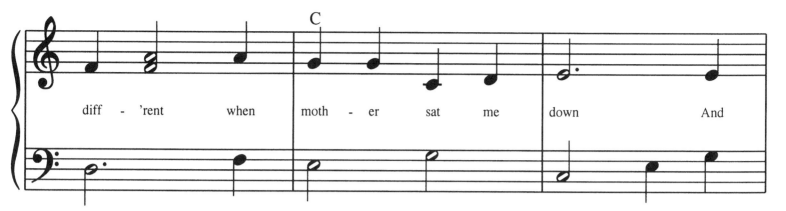

diff - 'rent when moth - er sat me down And

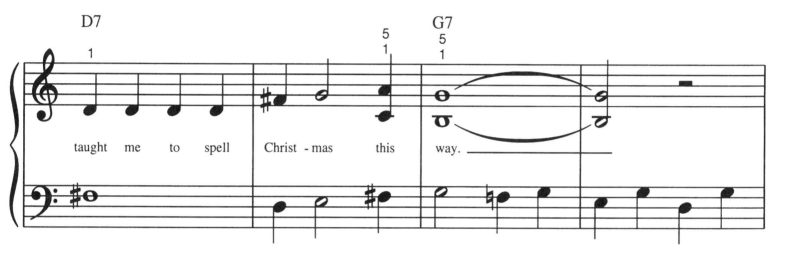

taught me to spell Christ - mas this way. _____

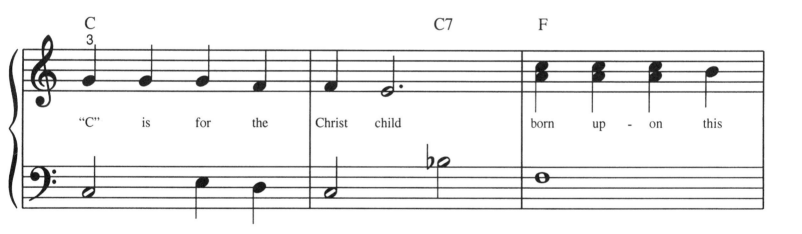

"C" is for the Christ child born up - on this

day. "H" for her - ald an - gels in the

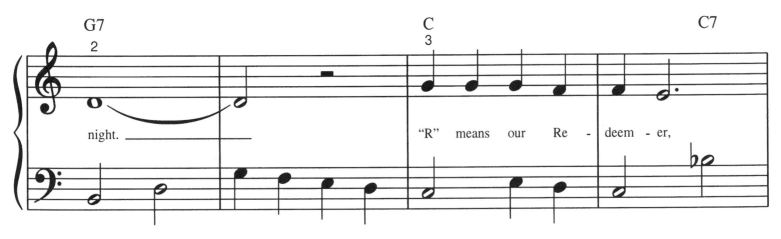

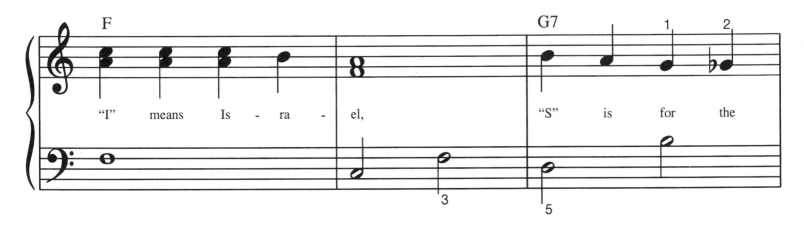

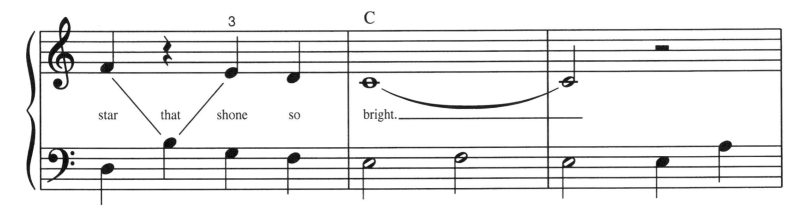

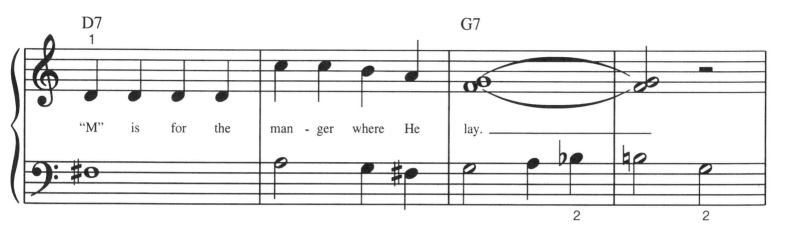

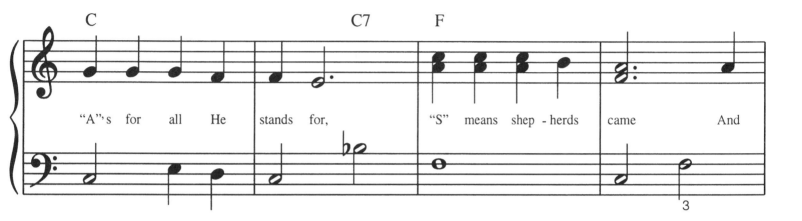

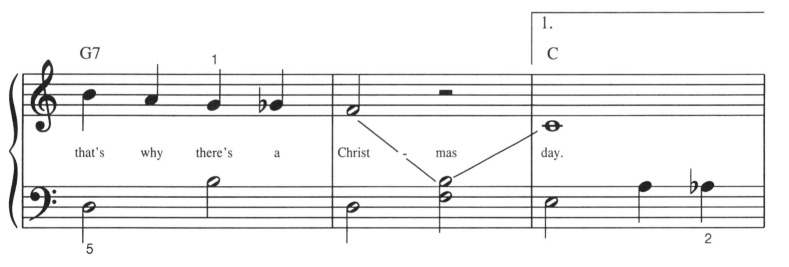

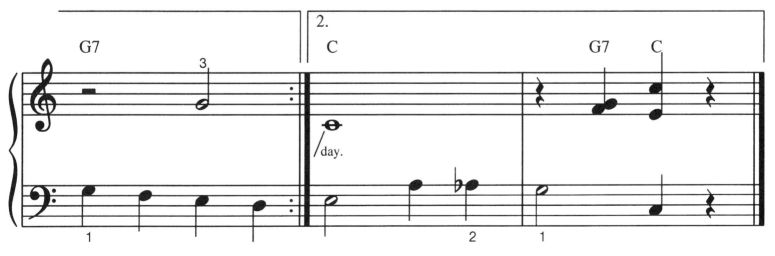

THE CHRISTMAS SONG
(Chestnuts Roasting on an Open Fire)

Music and Lyric by MEL TORME
and ROBERT WELLS

Slowly

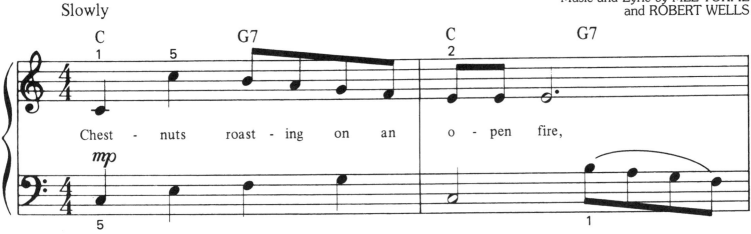

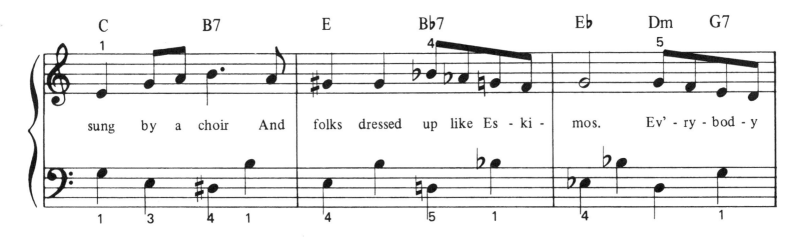

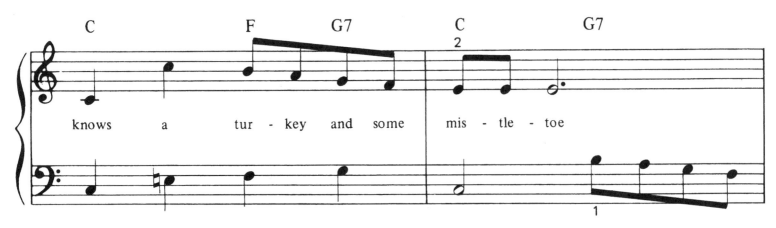

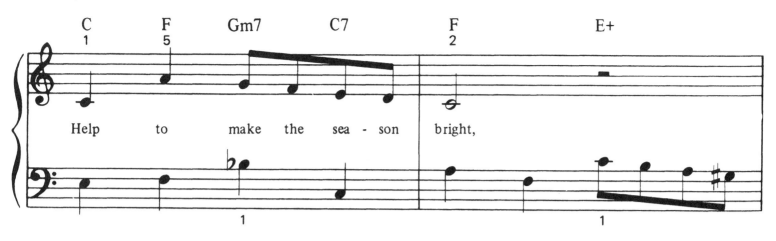

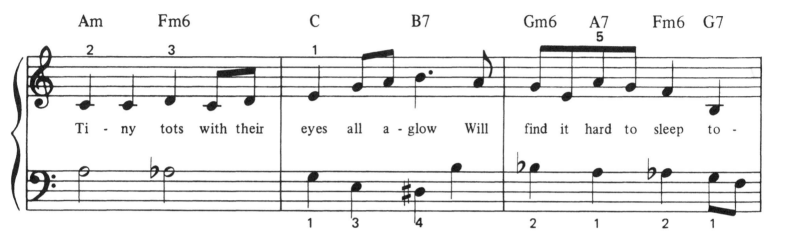

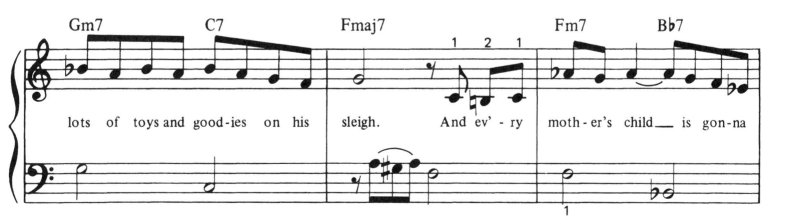

spy___ To see if rein-deer real - ly know how to fly. And

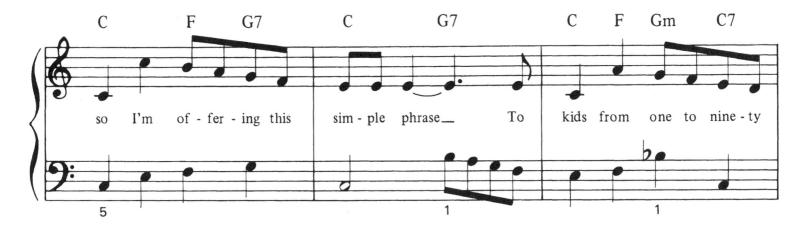

so I'm of - fer - ing this sim - ple phrase___ To kids from one to nine - ty

two; Al - though it's been said man - y times, man - y ways, "Mer - ry

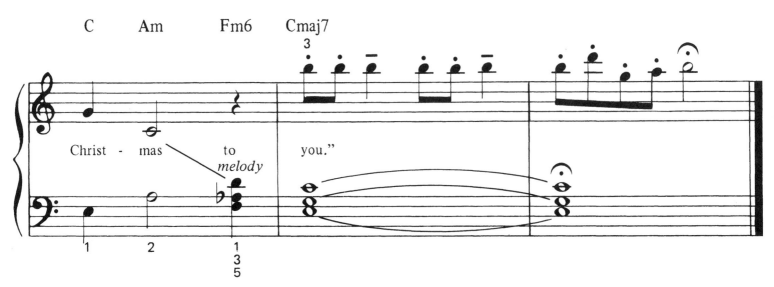

Christ - mas to *melody* you."

THE CHRISTMAS WALTZ

Words by SAMMY CAHN
Music by JULE STYNE

Graceful Waltz

Frost - ed

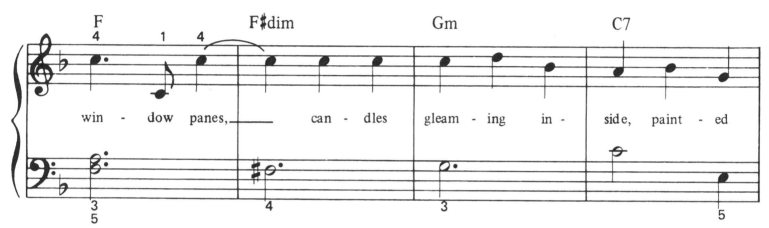

win - dow panes,___ can - dles gleam - ing in - side, paint - ed

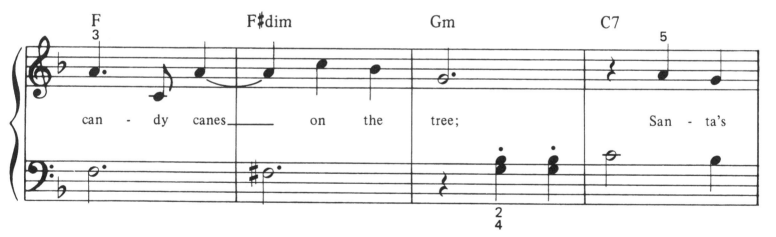

can - dy canes___ on the tree; San - ta's

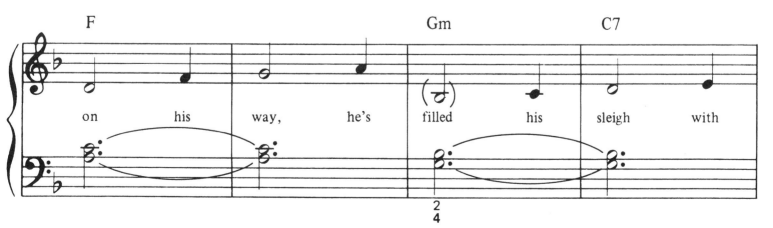

on his way, he's filled his sleigh with

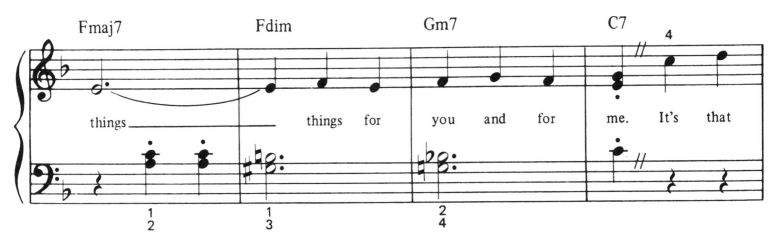

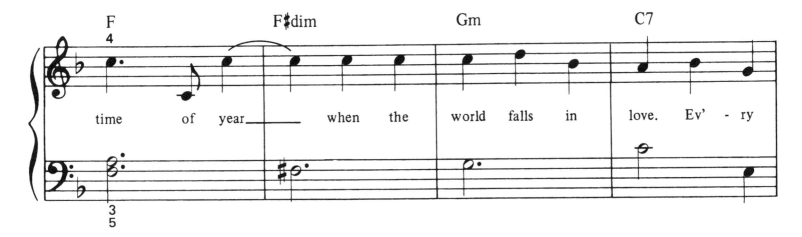

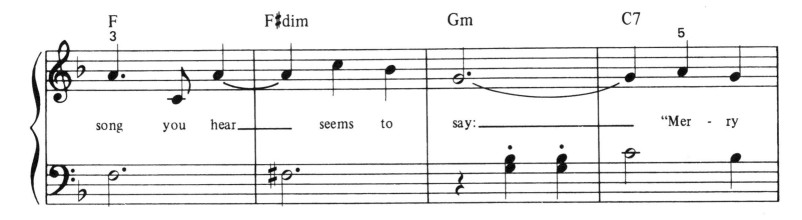

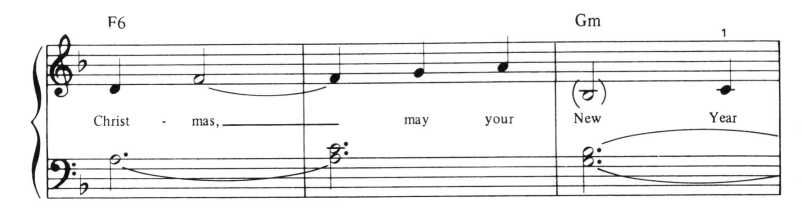

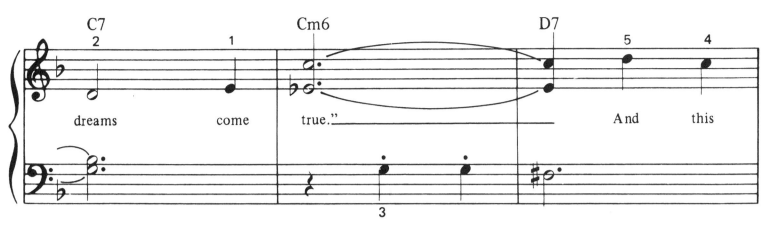

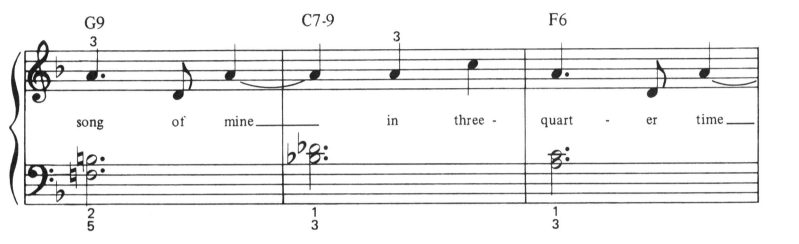

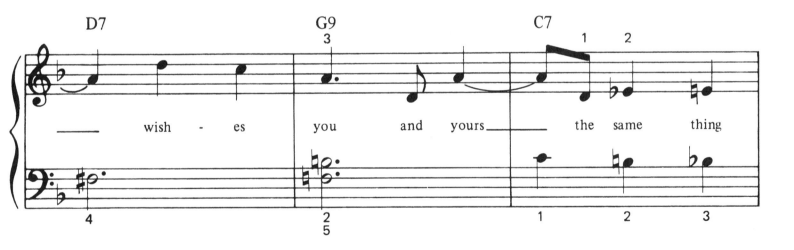

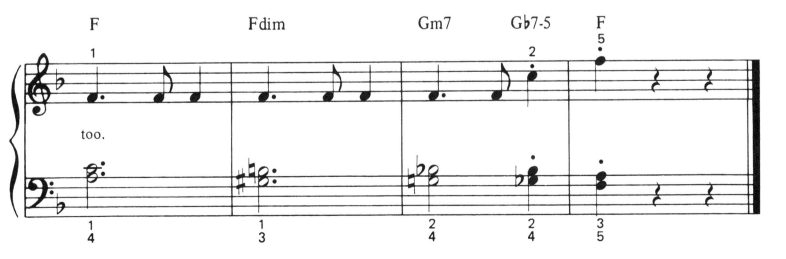

COME, THOU LONG EXPECTED JESUS

Words by CHARLES WESLEY
Music by ROWLAND HUGH PRICHARD

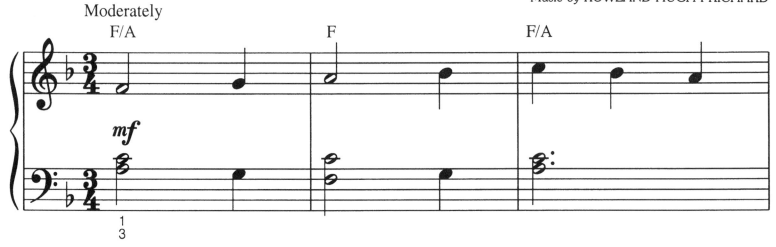

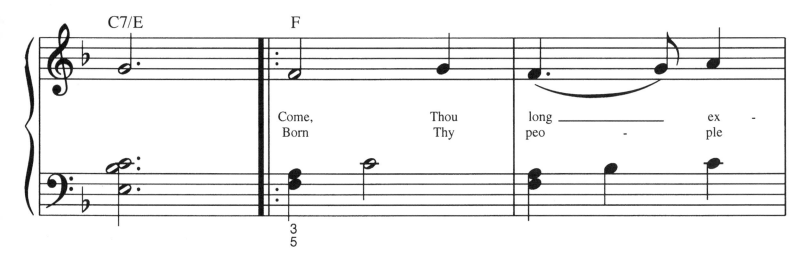

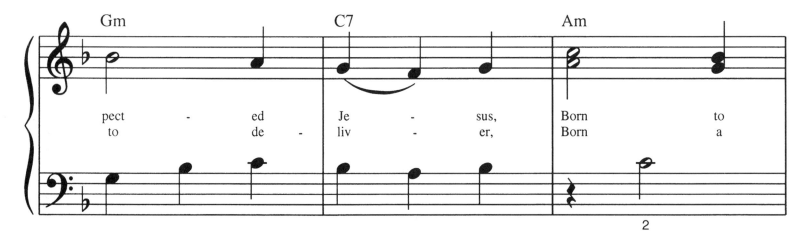

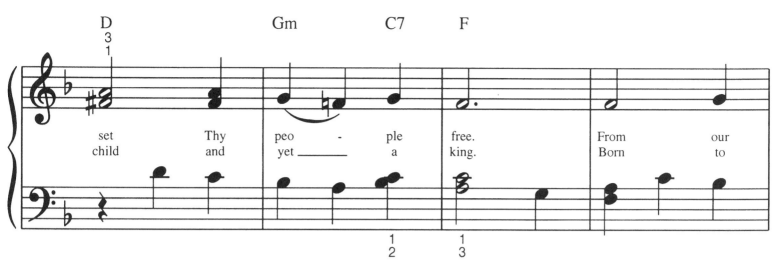

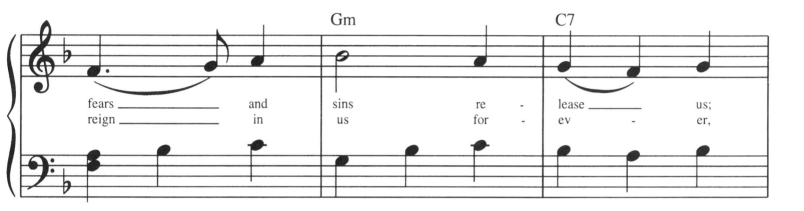

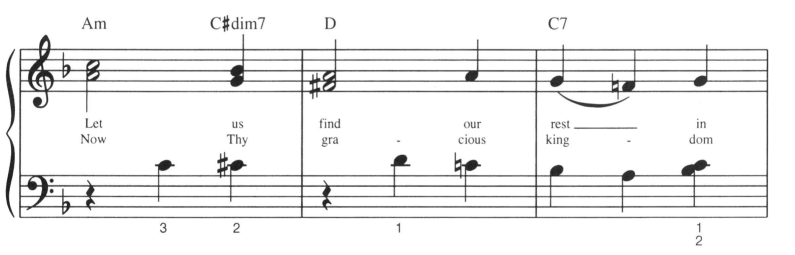

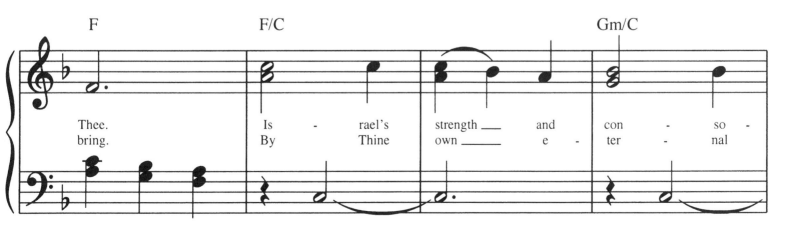

28

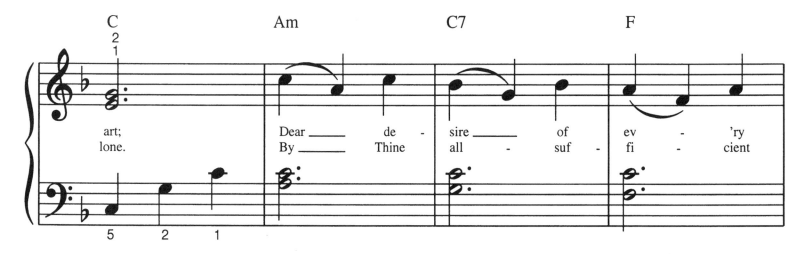

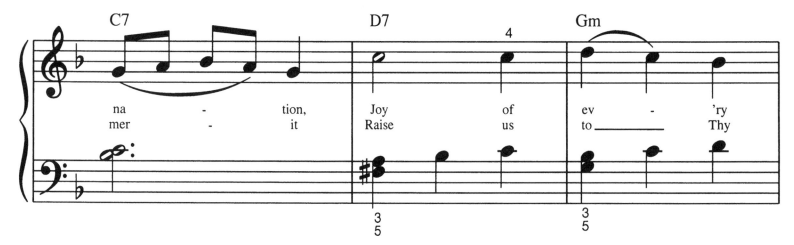

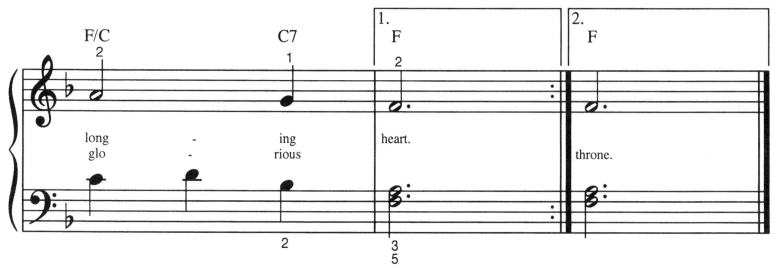

COVENTRY CAROL

Words by ROBERT CROO
Traditional English Melody

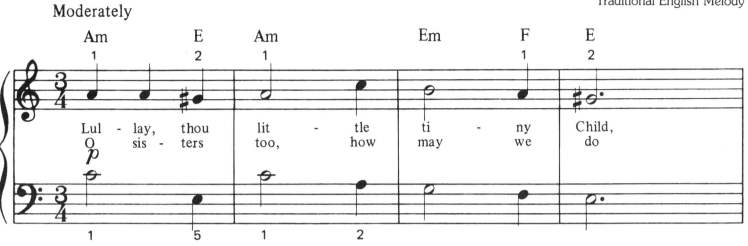

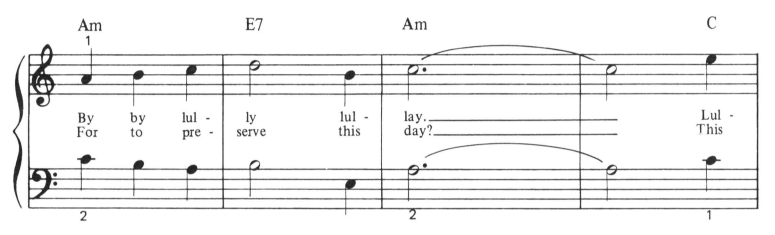

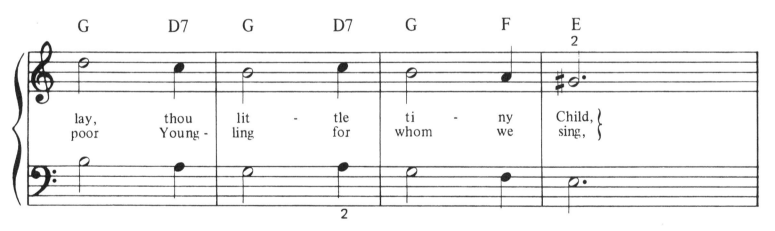

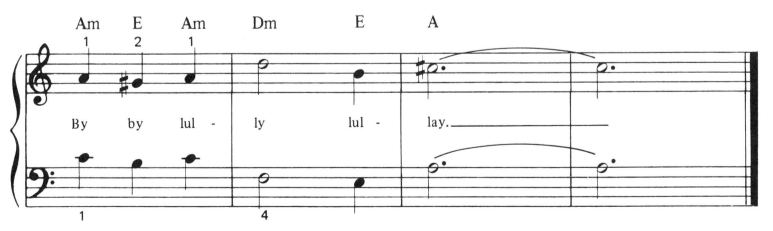

DECK THE HALL

Traditional Welsh Carol

Moderately

Deck   the hall   with   boughs of   hol - ly
See   the blaz - ing   yule be - fore   us,

Fa la la la la,   la   la la la.   'Tis   the sea - son
Fa la la la la,   la   la la la.   Strike   the harp and

to   be jol - ly   Fa la la la la,   la   la la la.
join the cho - rus.   Fa la la la la,   la   la la la.

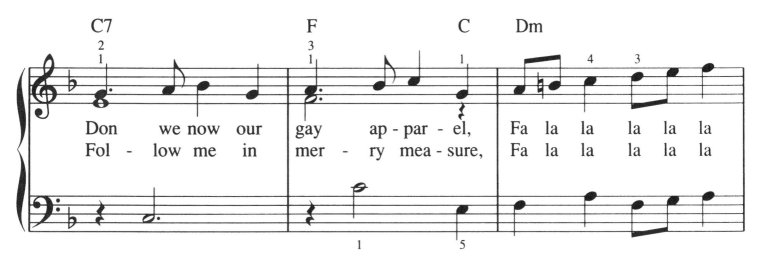

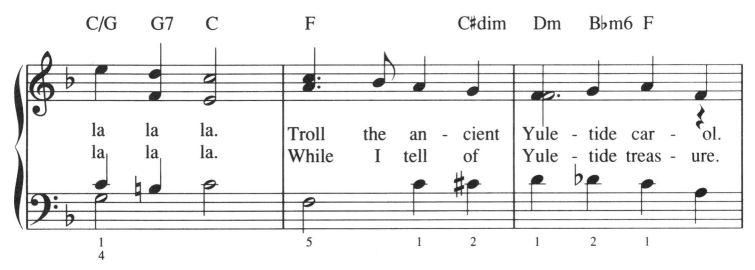

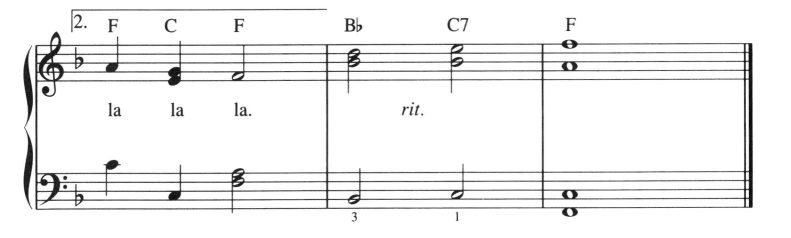

DING DONG! MERRILY ON HIGH!

French Carol

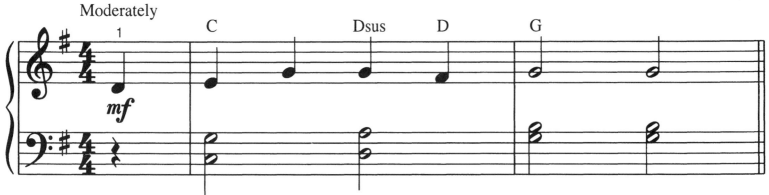

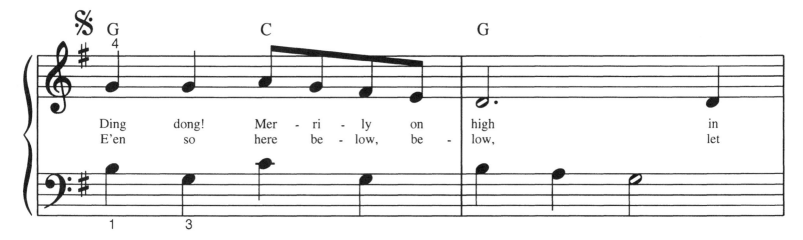

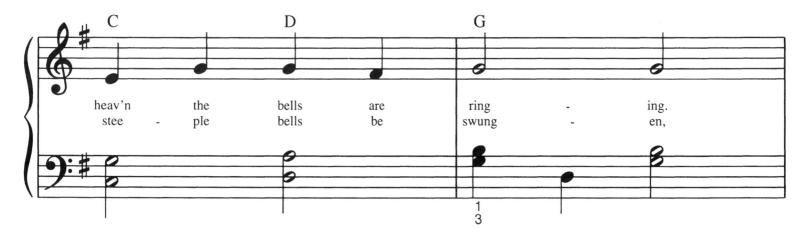

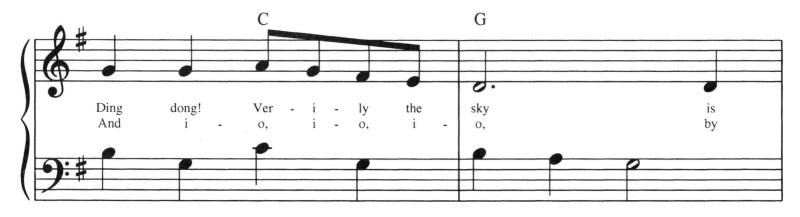

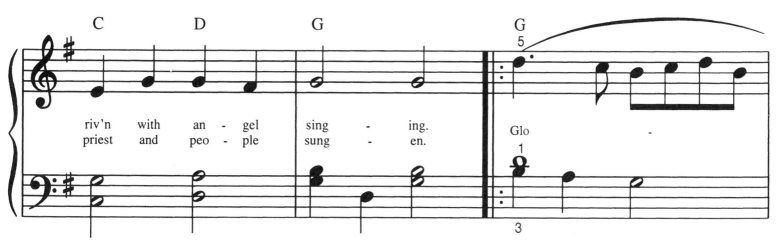

riv'n   with   an - gel   sing - - ing.
priest   and   peo - ple   sung - en.

Glo -

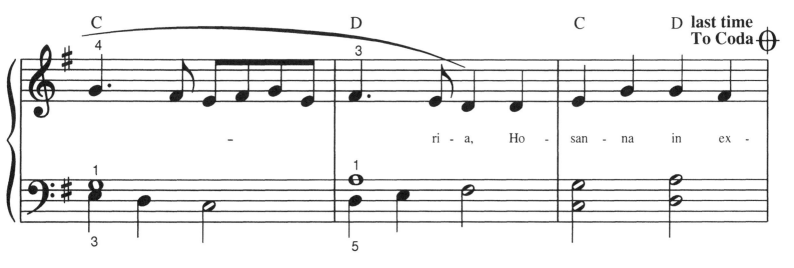

ri - a,   Ho - san - na   in   ex -

last time
To Coda

1.,3.
cel - sis!

2.
cel - sis!

D.S. al Coda

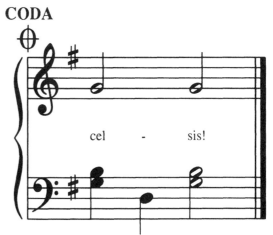

CODA
cel - sis!

THE FIRST NOEL

17th Century English Carol

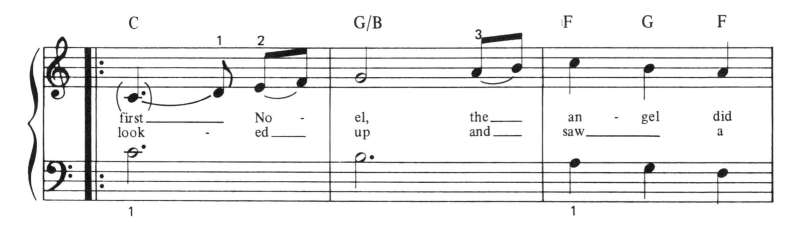

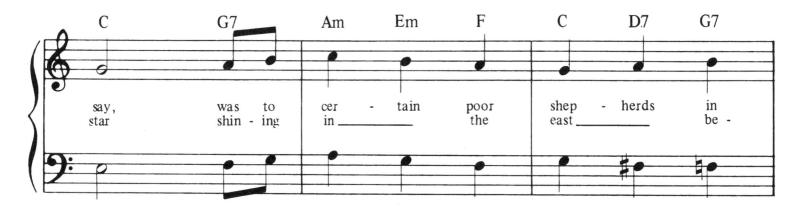

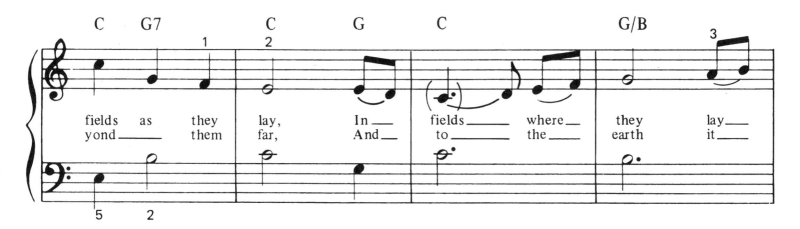

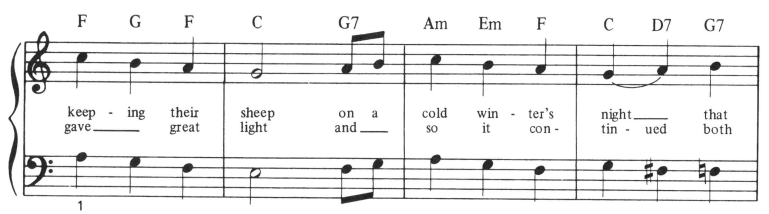

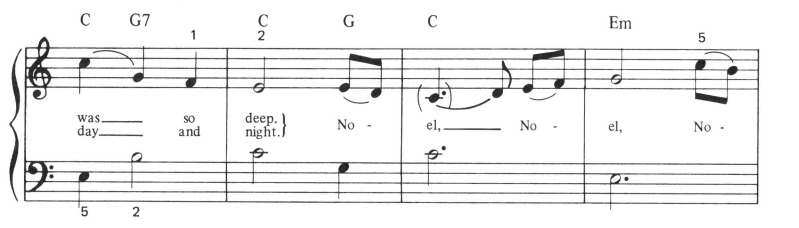

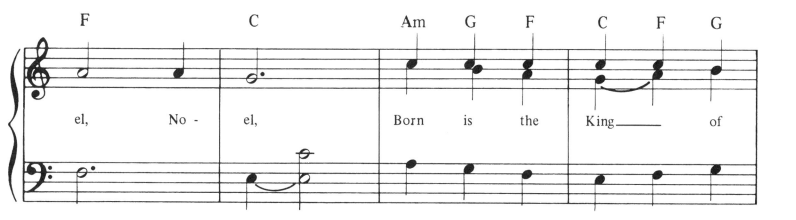

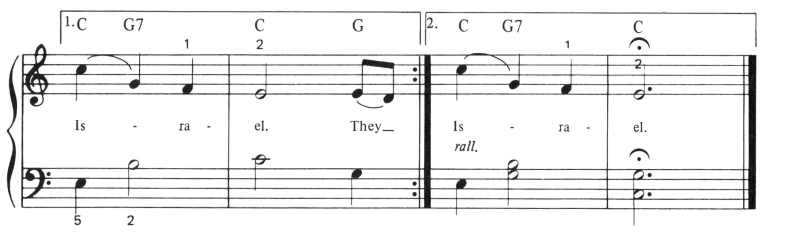

THE FRIENDLY BEASTS

Traditional English Carol

Gently

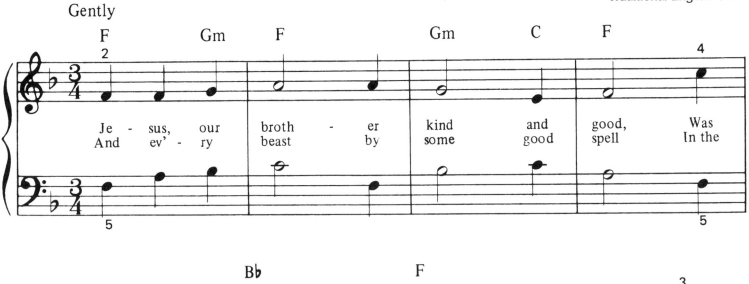

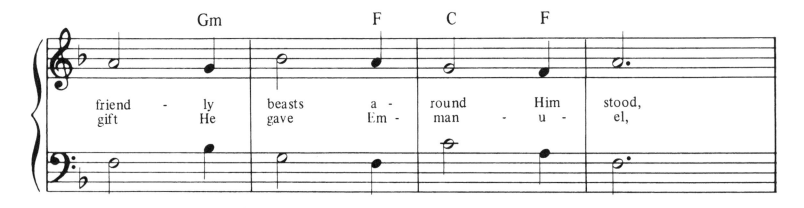

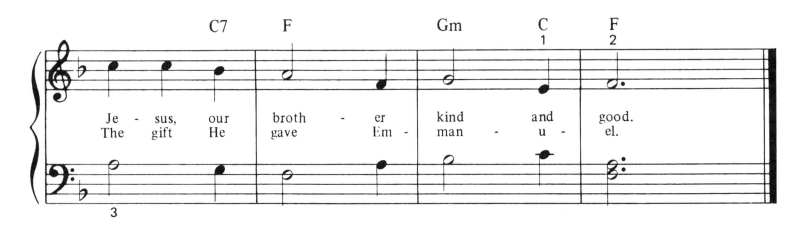

FROSTY THE SNOW MAN

Words and Music by STEVE NELSON
and JACK ROLLINS

Fros - ty the Snow Man was a jol - ly hap - py
Fros - ty the Snow Man knew the sun was hot that

soul, With a corn cob pipe and a but - ton nose and two
day, So he said "Let's run and we'll have some fun now be -

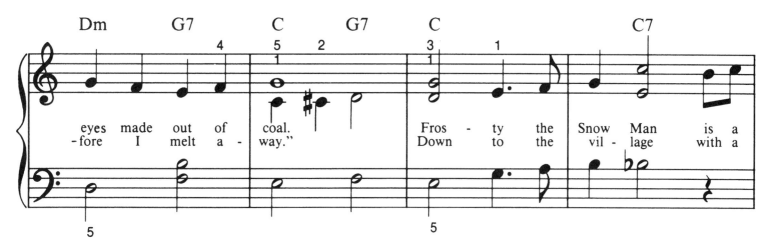

eyes made out of coal." Fros - ty the Snow Man is a
-fore I melt a - way." Down to the vil - lage with a

fair - y tale they say,
broom - stick in his hand,
He was made of snow but the
Run - ning here and there all a -

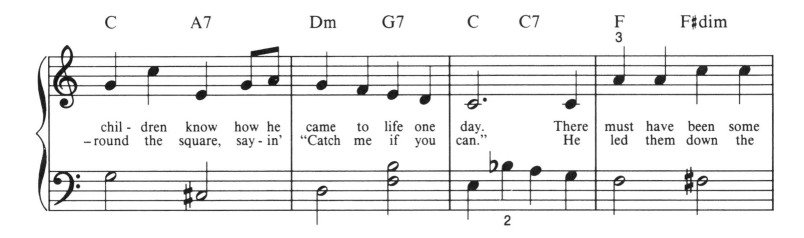

chil - dren know how he came to life one day.
-round the square, say - in' "Catch me if you can."
There must have been some
He led them down the

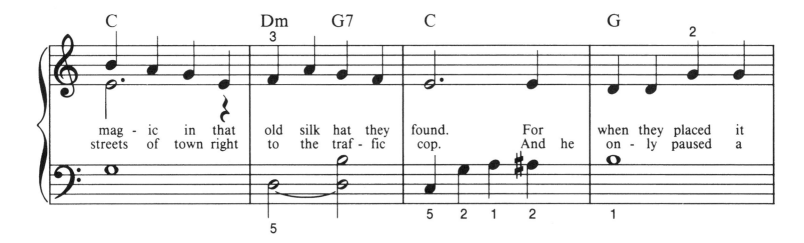

mag - ic in that old silk hat they found. For
streets of town right to the traf - fic cop. And he
when they placed it
on - ly paused a

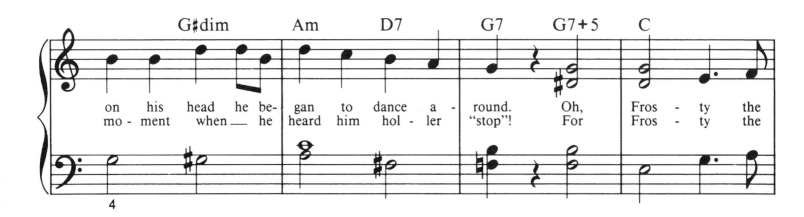

on his head he be - gan to dance a - round. Oh,
mo - ment when — he heard him hol - ler "stop"! For
Fros - ty the
Fros - ty the

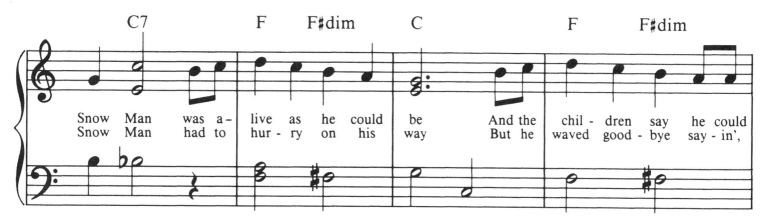

Snow Man was a- live as he could be And the chil - dren say he could
Snow Man had to hur - ry on his way But he waved good - bye say - in',

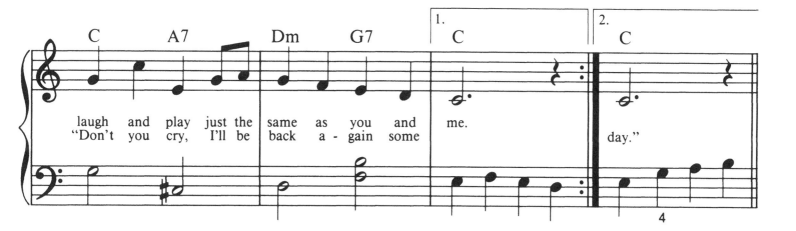

laugh and play just the same as you and me.
"Don't you cry, I'll be back a - gain some day."

Thump-et - y thump thump, thump-et - y thump thump Look at Fros - ty go.

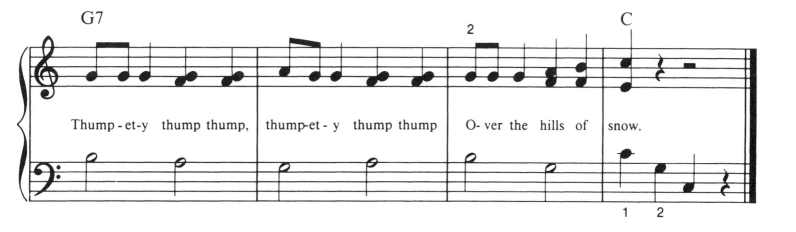

Thump-et-y thump thump, thump-et-y thump thump O- ver the hills of snow.

GO TELL IT ON THE MOUNTAIN

African-American Spiritual

Go, tell it on the moun - tain

O - ver the hills and ev - ery - where, Go, tell it on the

moun - tain that Je - sus Christ __ is born. The

shep - herds feared and trem - bled When lo! a - bove the

41

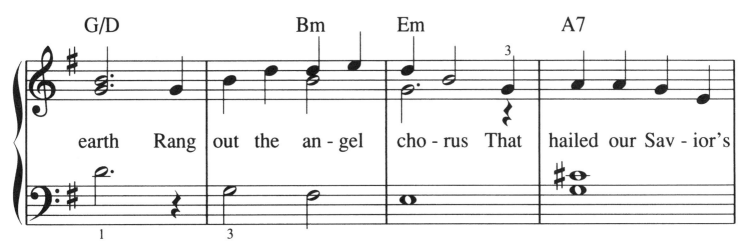

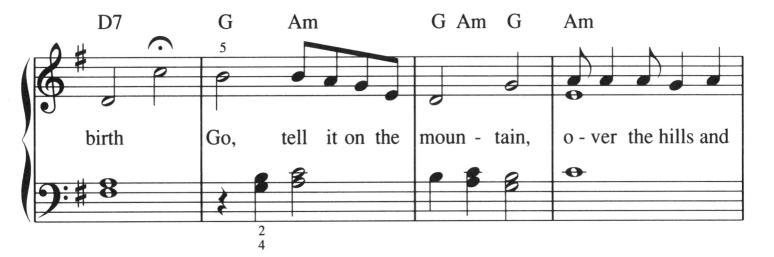

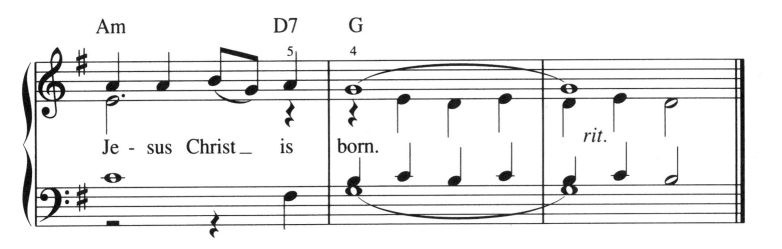

GOOD CHRISTIAN MEN, REJOICE

14th Century German Melody

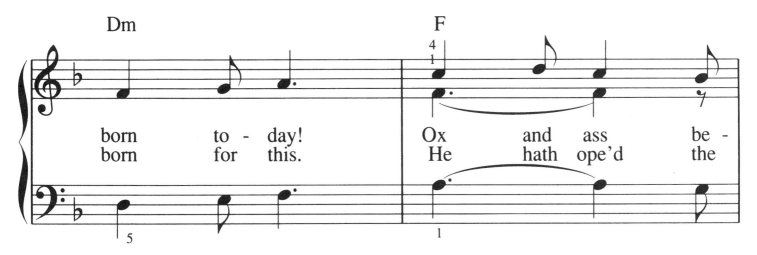

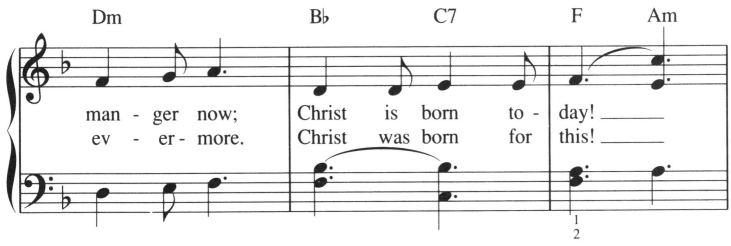

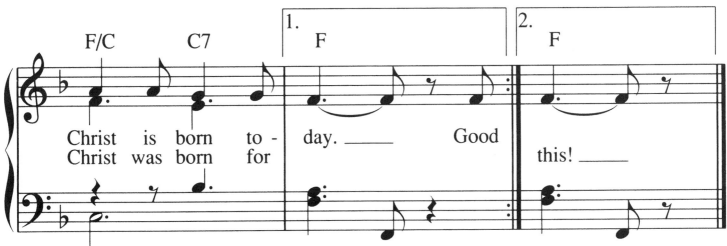

GOOD KING WENCESLAS

Words by JOHN M. NEALE
Music by PIAE CANTIONES

GRANDMA GOT RUN OVER BY A REINDEER

Words and Music by
RANDY BROOKS

CHORUS:

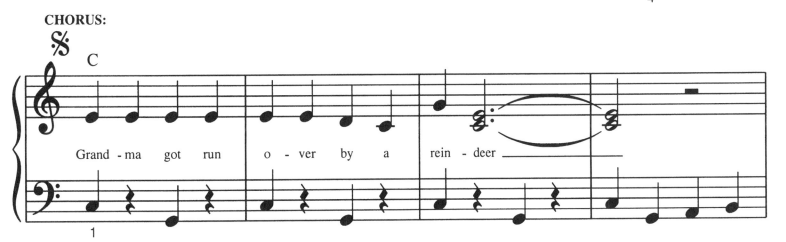

Grand - ma got run o - ver by a rein - deer

walk - ing home from our house Christ - mas Eve.

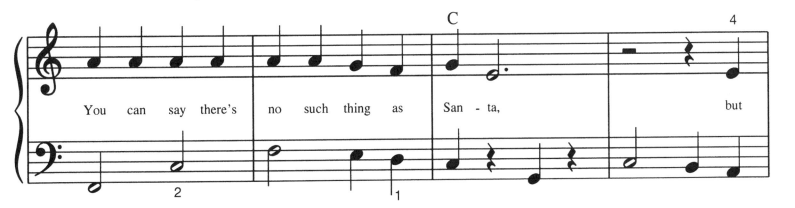

You can say there's no such thing as San - ta, but

as for me and Grand-pa, we be-lieve.

VERSE:

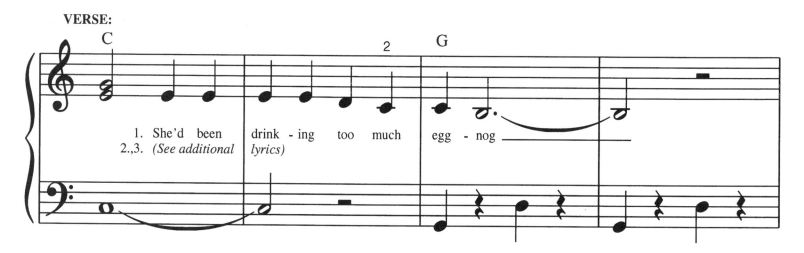

1. She'd been drink-ing too much egg-nog
2.,3. *(See additional lyrics)*

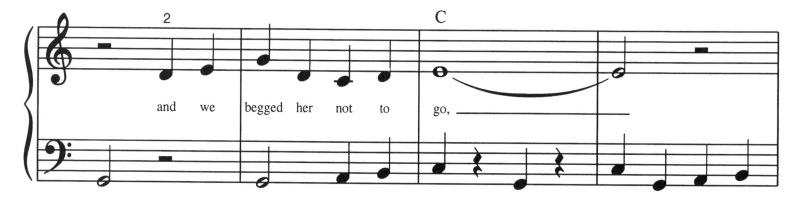

and we begged her not to go, ___

but she for-got her med-i-ca-tion, and she

stag - gered out the door in - to the snow.

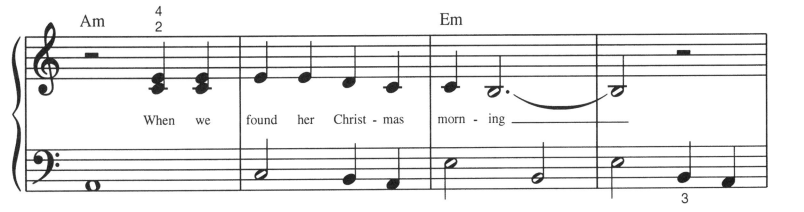

When we found her Christ - mas morn - ing

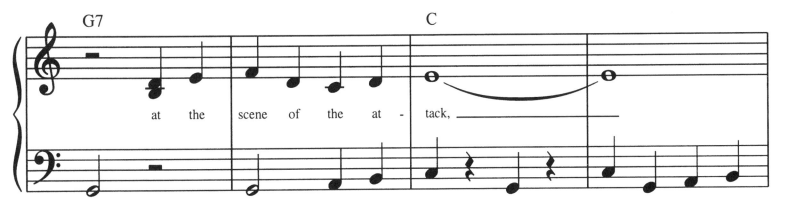

at the scene of the at - tack,

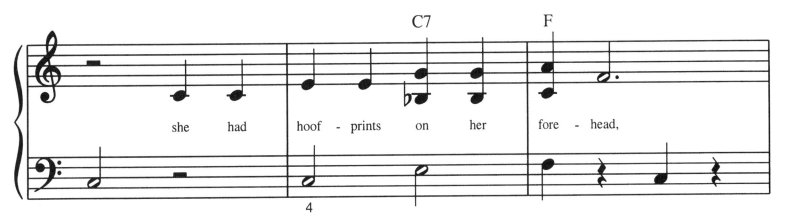

she had hoof - prints on her fore - head,

and in- crim- i- nat- ing Claus marks on her back.

1st and 2nd time D.S.
3rd time D.S. al Coda

CODA

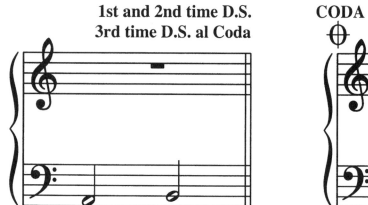

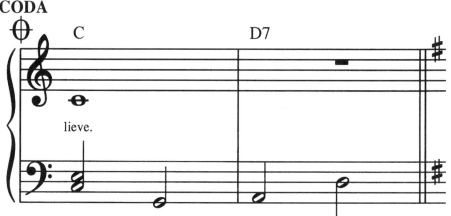

lieve.

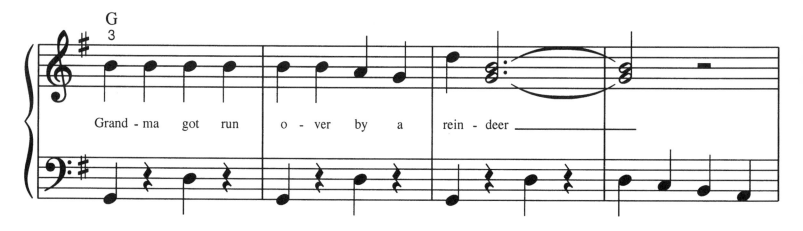

Grand- ma got run o- ver by a rein- deer

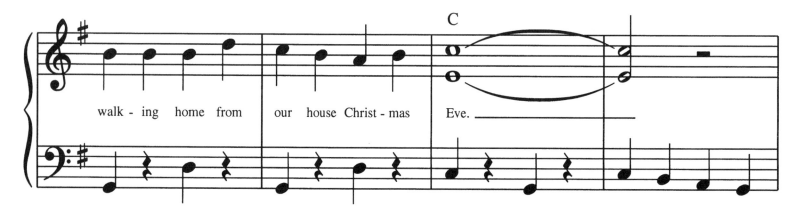

walk- ing home from our house Christ- mas Eve.

You can say there's no such thing as San - ta,

but as for me and Grand - pa, we be - lieve.

Additional Lyrics

2. Now we're all so proud of Grandpa,
   He's been taking this so well.
   See him in there watching football,
   Drinking beer and playing cards with Cousin Mel.
   It's not Christmas without Grandma.
   All the family's dressed in black,
   And we just can't help but wonder:
   Should we open up her gifts or send them back?
   To Chorus

3. Now the goose is on the table,
   And the pudding made of fig,
   And the blue and silver candles,
   That would just have matched the hair in Grandma's wig.
   I've warned all my friends and neighbors,
   Better watch out for yourselves.
   They should never give a license
   To a man who drives a sleigh and plays with elves.
   To Chorus

GRANDMA'S KILLER FRUITCAKE

Words and Music by ELMO SHROPSHIRE
and RITA ABRAMS

Moderately

The

hol-i-days were up-on us and things were go-in' fine, 'til the

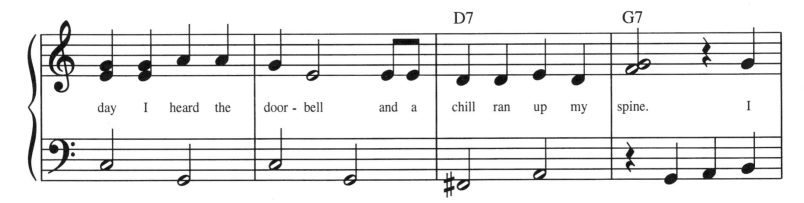

day I heard the door-bell and a chill ran up my spine. I

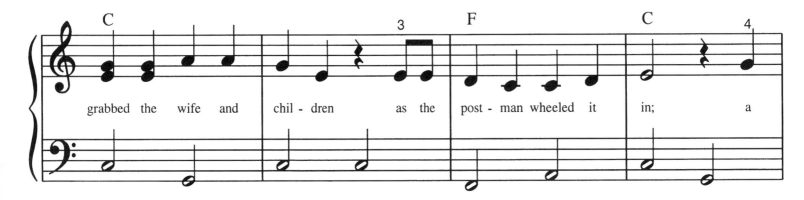

grabbed the wife and chil-dren as the post-man wheeled it in; a

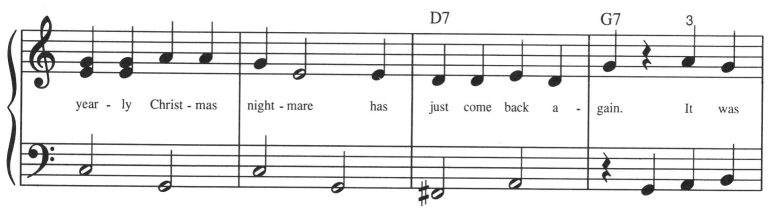

year - ly Christ - mas | night - mare has | just come back a - gain. | It was

hard - er than the head of | Un - cle Buck - y; | heav - y as a ser - mon of

Preach - er Luck - y; | One's e - nough to give the whole | state of Ken - tuck - y a

great big bel - ly | ache! It was | dens - er than a drove of | barn - yard tur - keys;

tough- er than a truck - load of all - beef jerk - y; dri - er than a drought in

Al - bu - quer -que; Grand - ma's kill - er fruit - cake!

Grand-ma's kill - er fruit - cake!

HAPPY HOLIDAY
from the Motion Picture Irving Berlin's HOLIDAY INN

Words and Music by
IRVING BERLIN

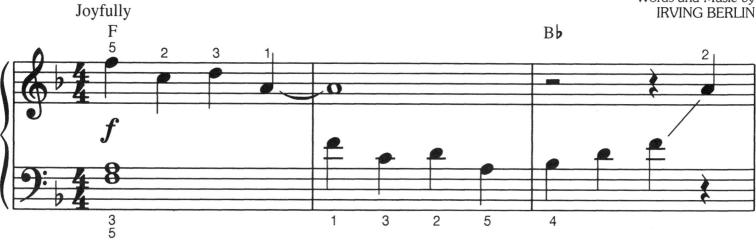

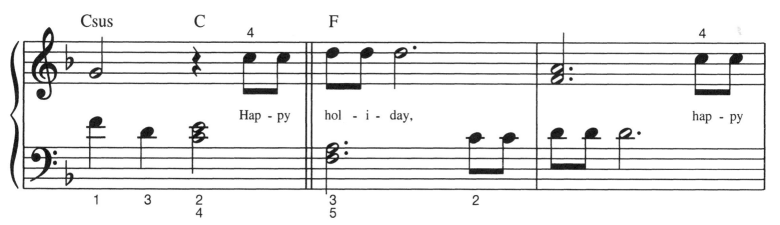

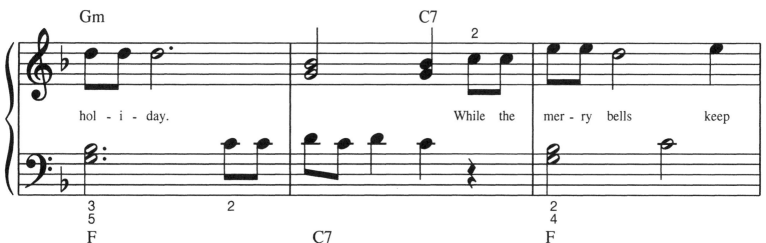

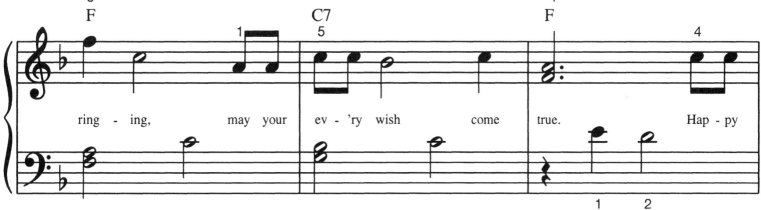

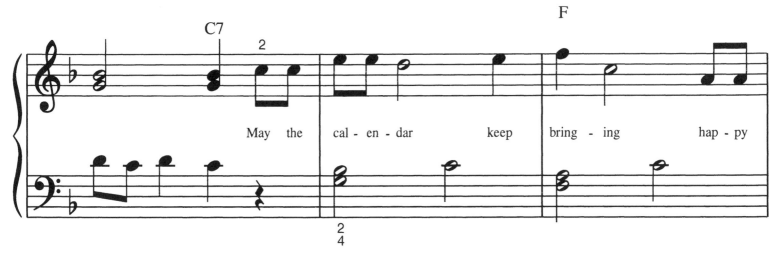

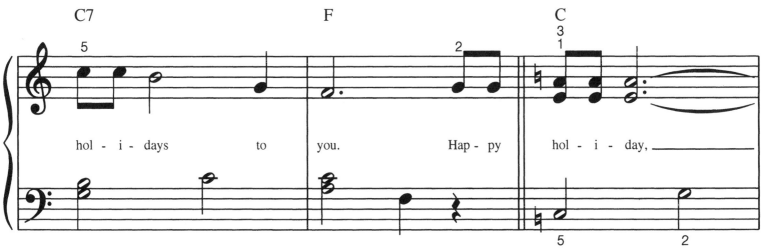

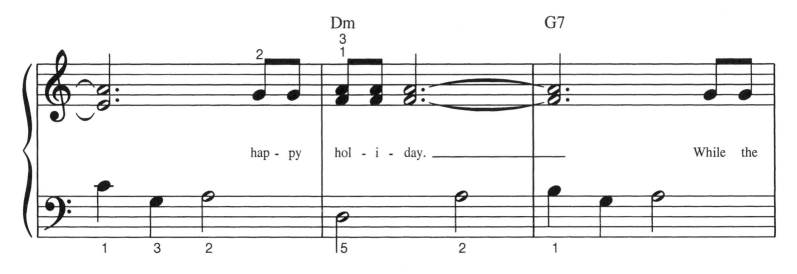

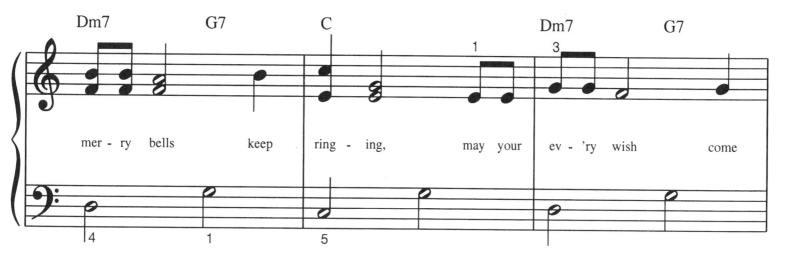

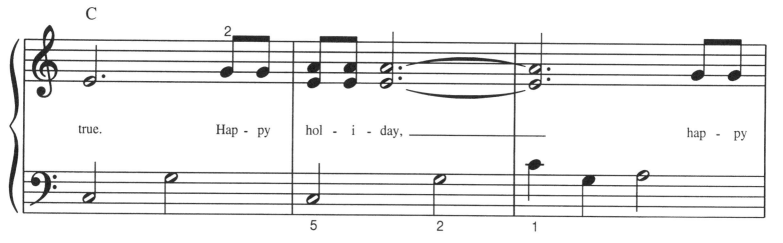

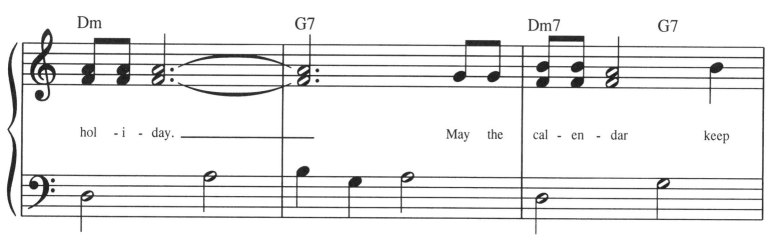

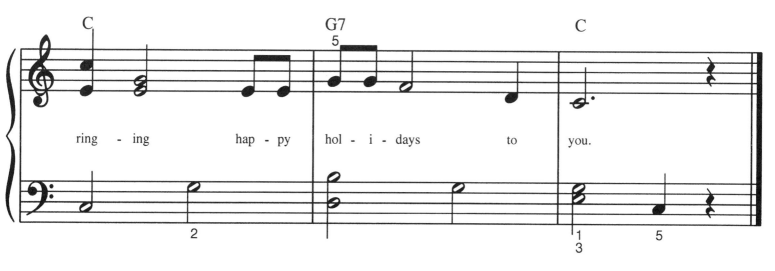

HARK! THE HERALD ANGELS SING

Words by CHARLES WESLEY
Music by FELIX MENDELSSOHN-BARTHOLDY

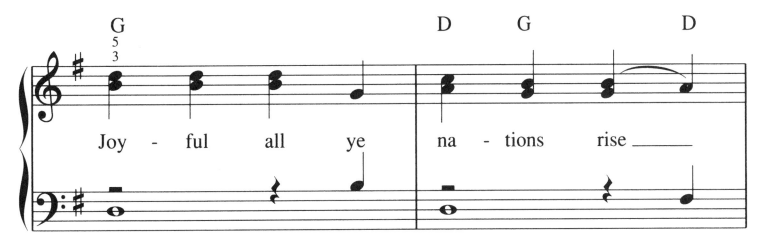

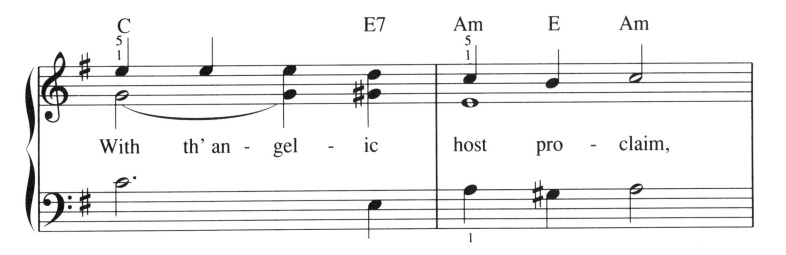

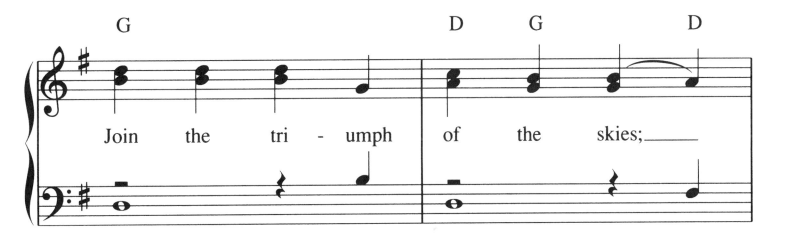

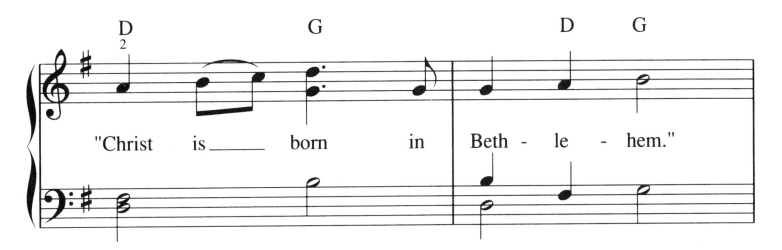

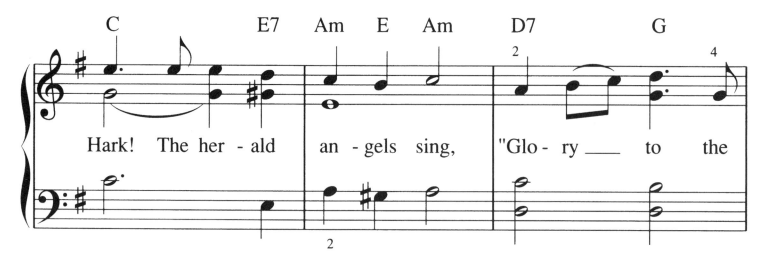

Hark! The her - ald an - gels sing, "Glo - ry ___ to the

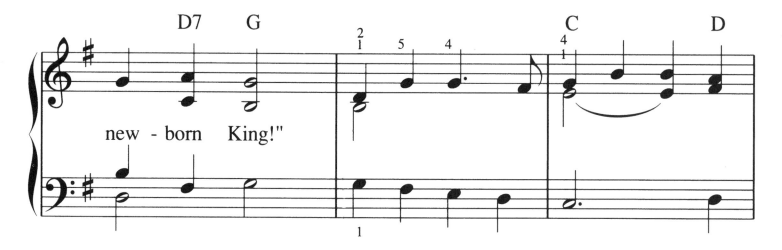

new - born King!"

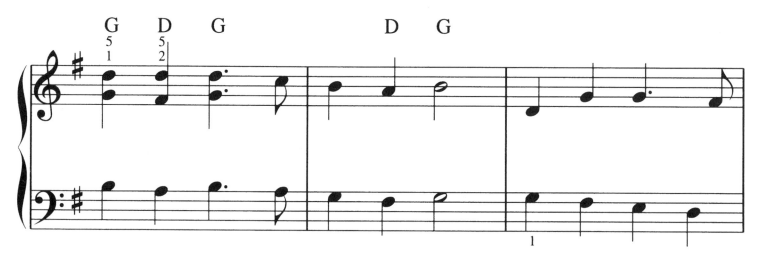

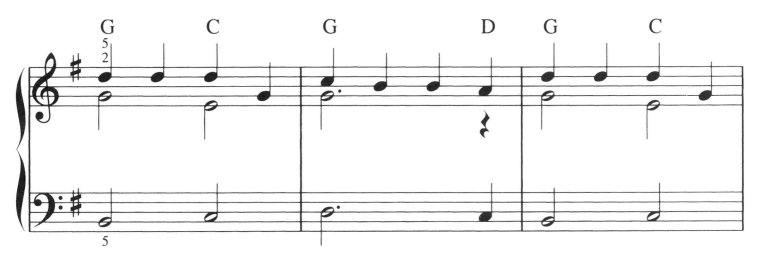

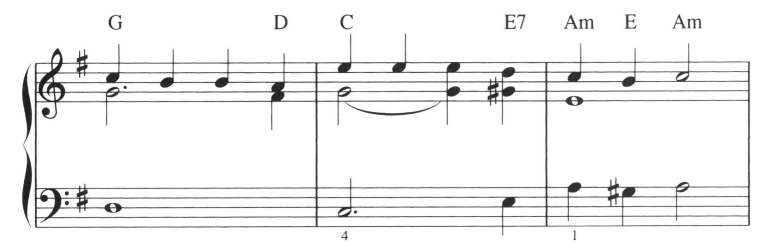

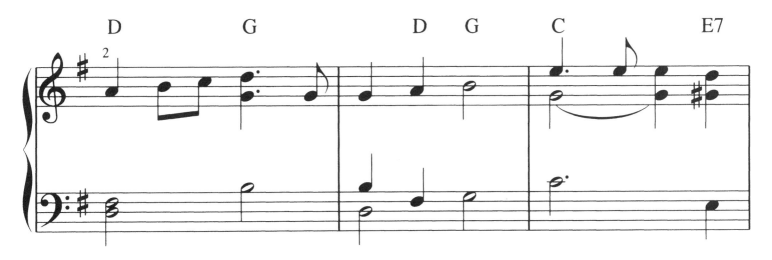

HE IS BORN

Traditional French Carol

He is born, the _____ ho - ly Child,

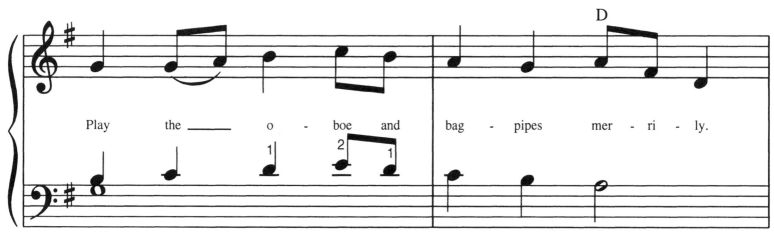

Play the _____ o - boe and bag - pipes mer - ri - ly.

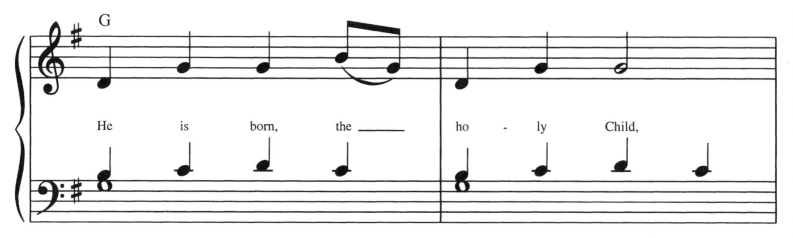

He is born, the _____ ho - ly Child,

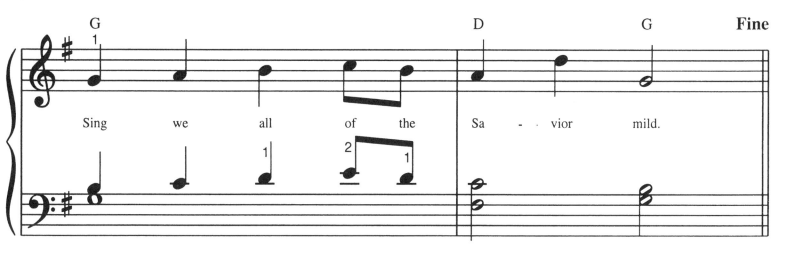

Sing we all of the Sa - vior mild.

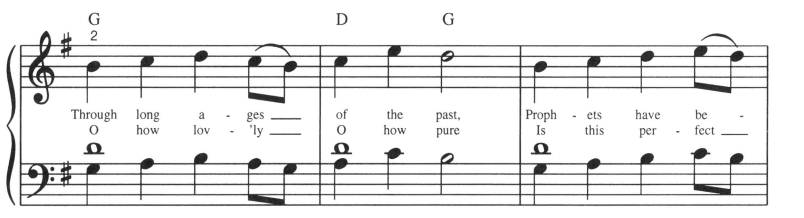

Through long a - ges ____ of the past, Proph - ets have be -
O how lov - 'ly ____ O how pure Is this per - fect ____

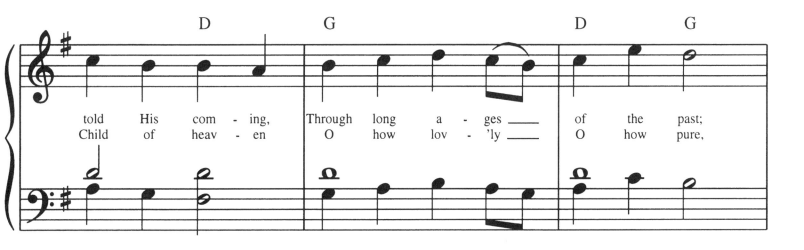

told His com - ing, Through long a - ges ____ of the past;
Child of heav - en O how lov - 'ly ____ O how pure,

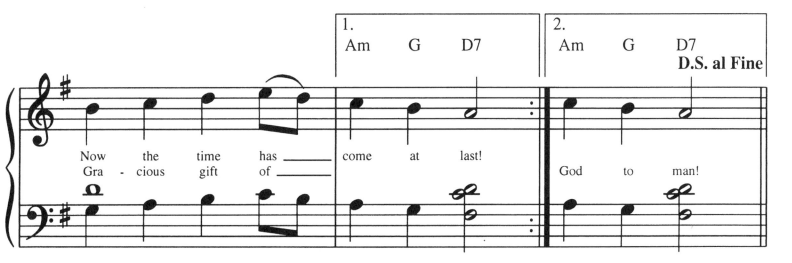

Now the time has ____ come at last!
Gra - cious gift of ____ God to man!

THE HOLLY AND THE IVY

18th Century English Carol

The

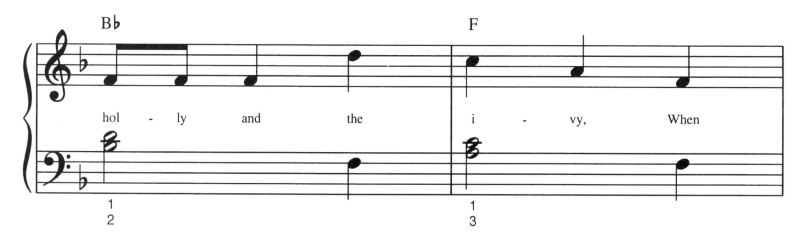

hol - ly and the i - vy, When

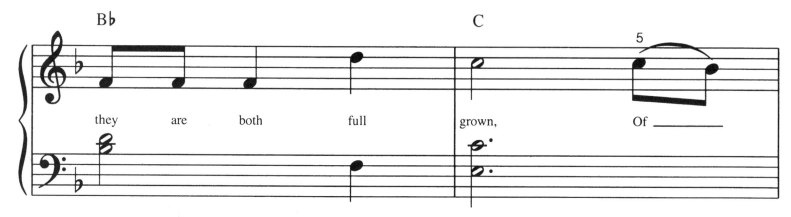

they are both full grown, Of

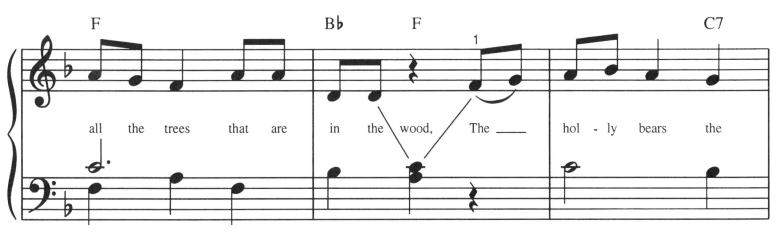

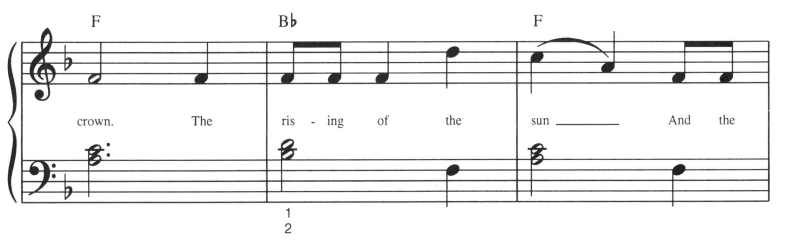

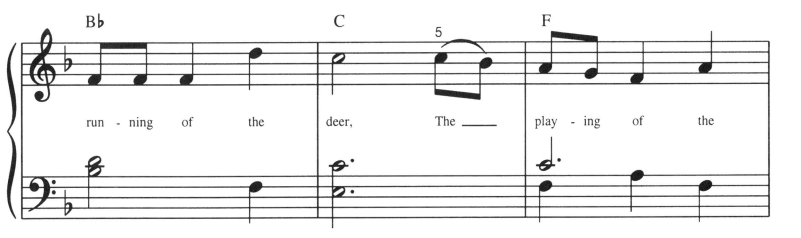

A HOLLY JOLLY CHRISTMAS

Music and Lyrics by
JOHNNY MARKS

Moderately Bright

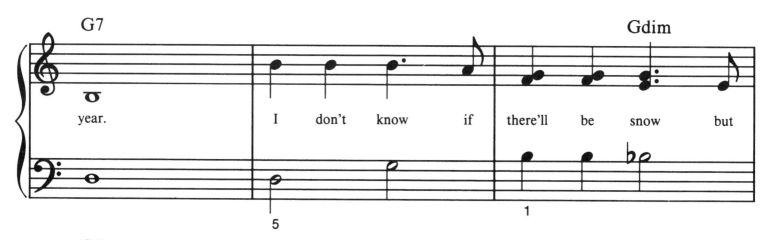

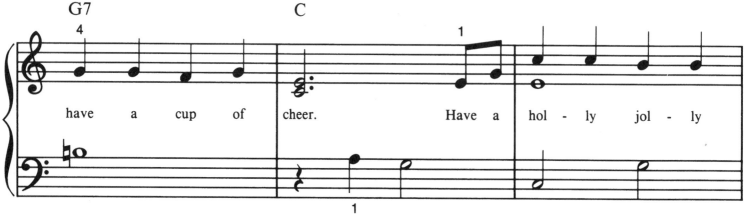

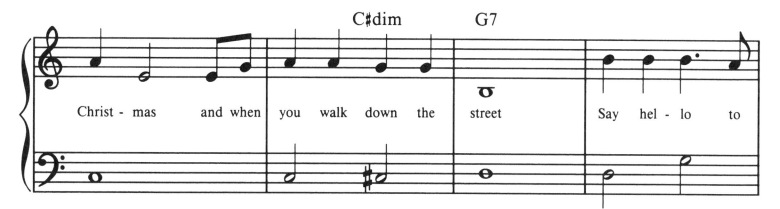

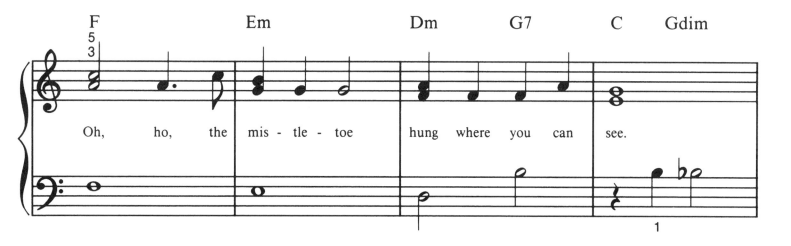

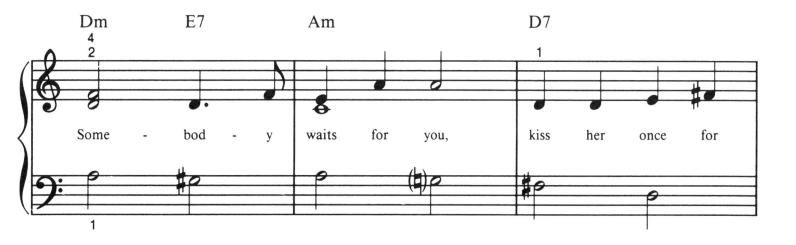

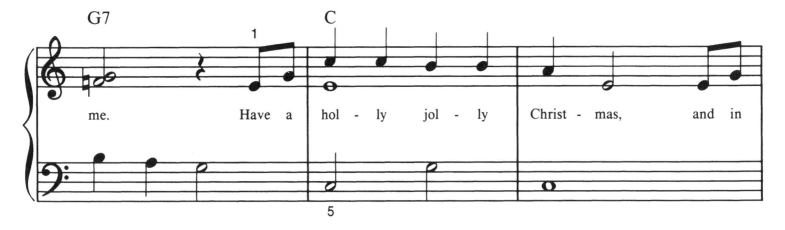

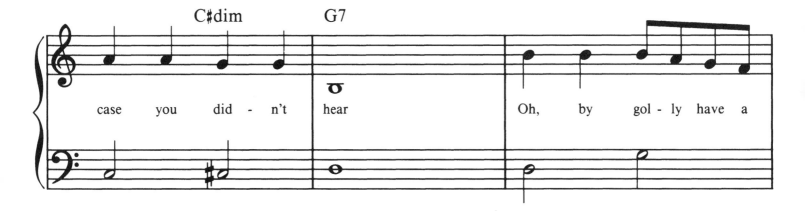

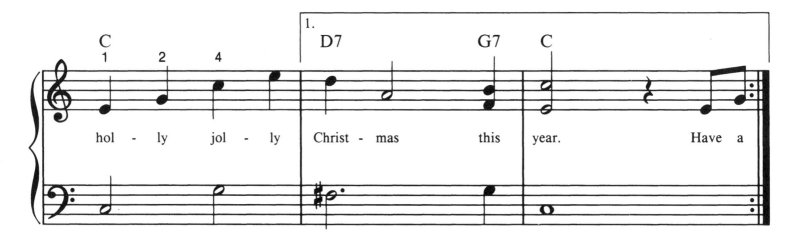

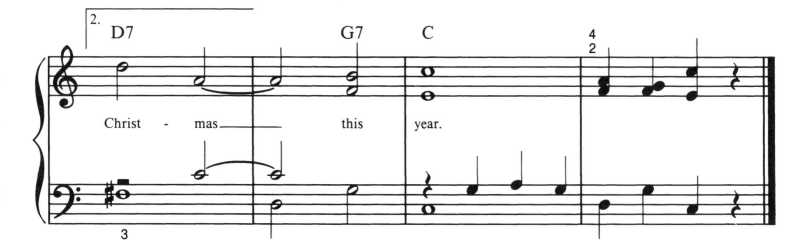

(There's No Place Like)
HOME FOR THE HOLIDAYS

Words by AL STILLMAN
Music by ROBERT ALLEN

Moderately

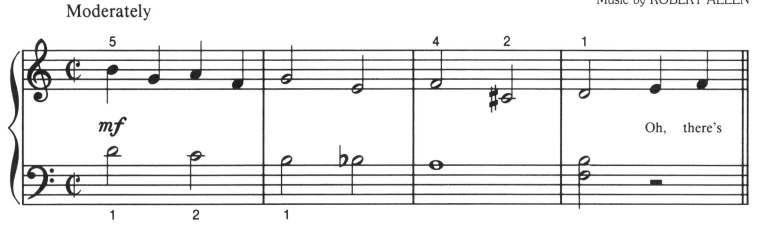

with pedal

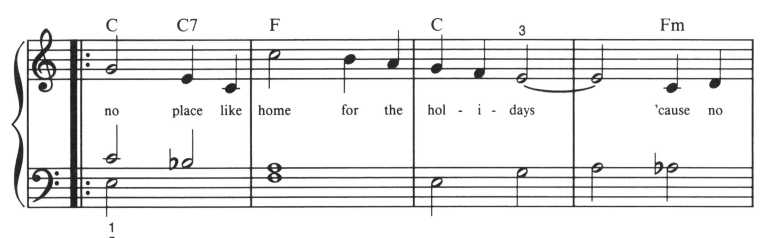

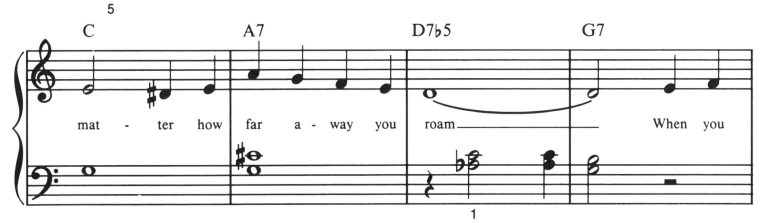

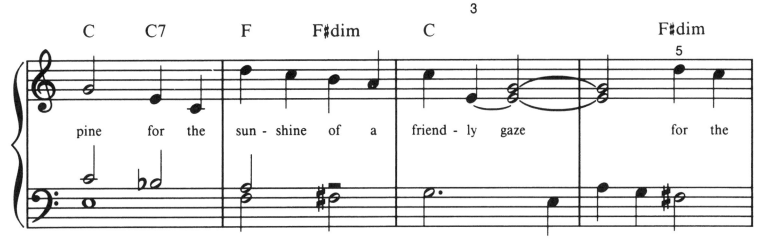

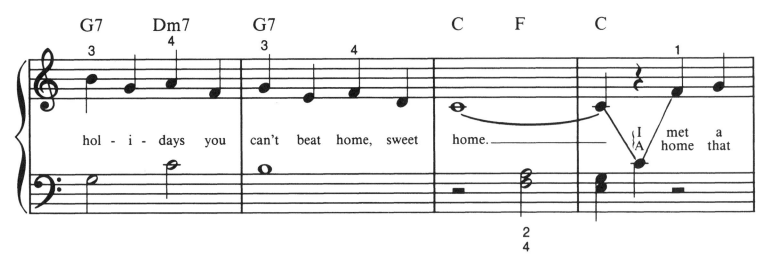

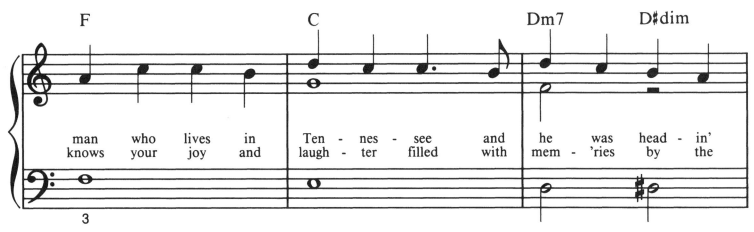

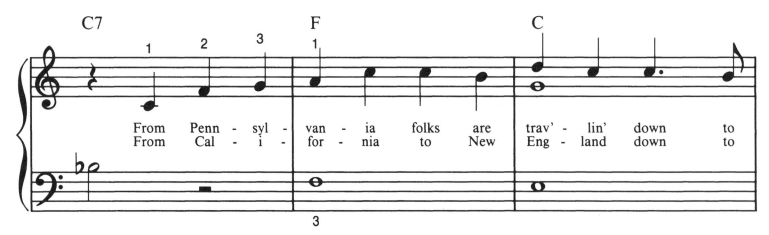

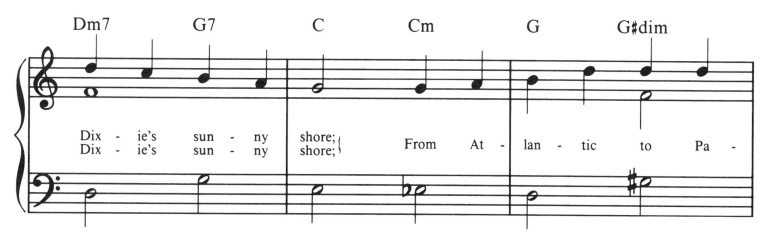

Dix - ie's sun - ny shore; { From At - lan - tic to Pa -
Dix - ie's sun - ny shore; {

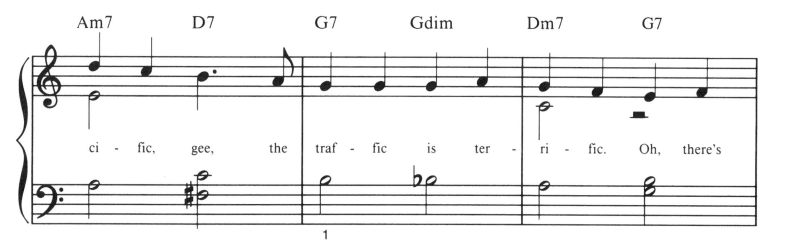

ci - fic, gee, the traf - fic is ter - ri - fic. Oh, there's

1

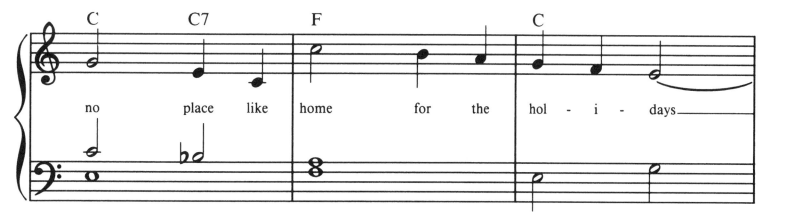

no place like home for the hol - i - days

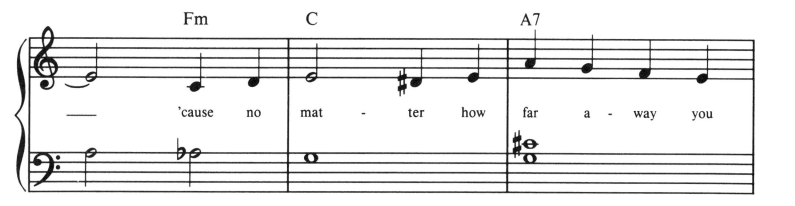

'cause no mat - ter how far a - way you

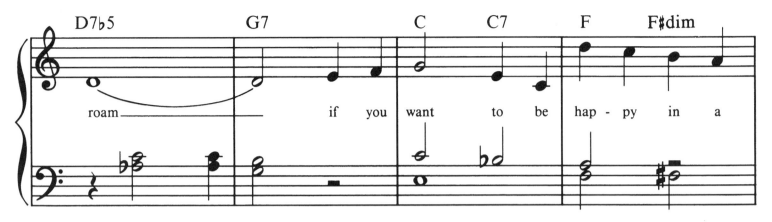

roam _____ if you want to be hap - py in a

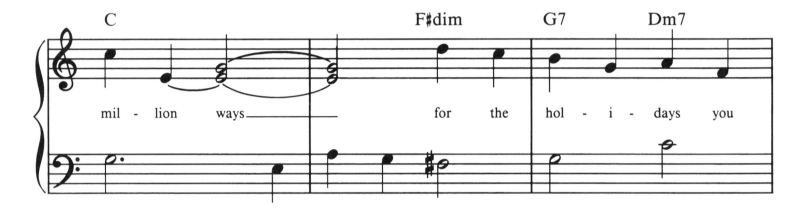

mil - lion ways _____ for the hol - i - days you

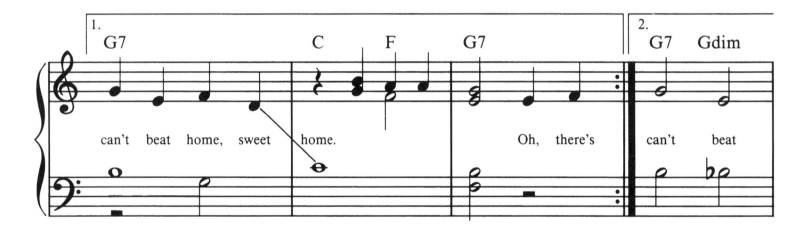

can't beat home, sweet home. Oh, there's | can't beat

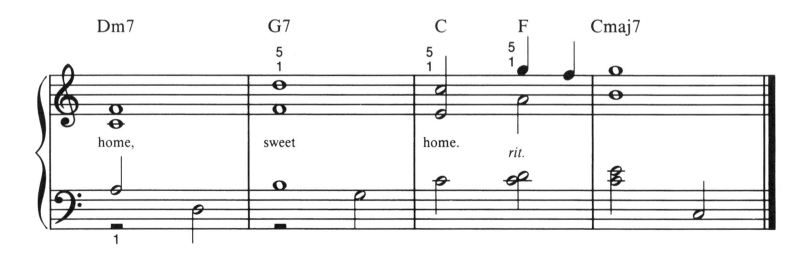

home, sweet home.
rit.

HYMNE

By VANGELIS

With pedal

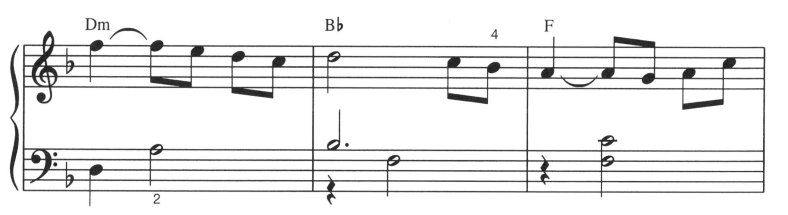

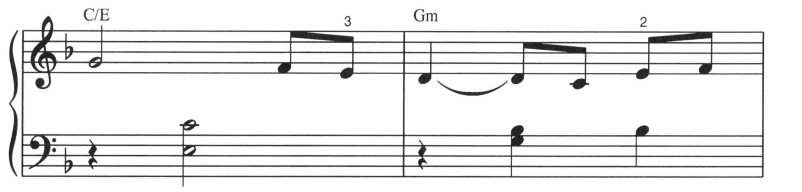

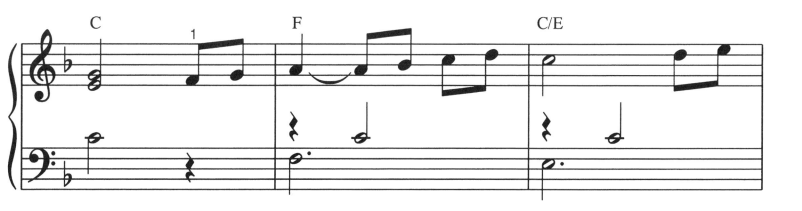

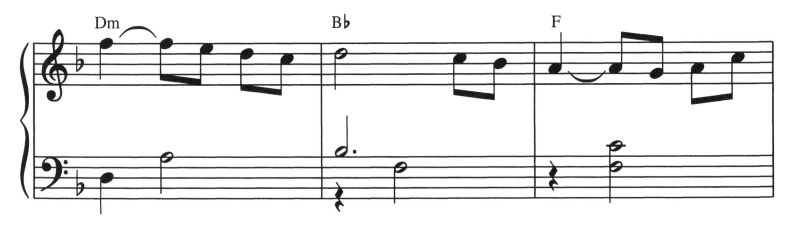

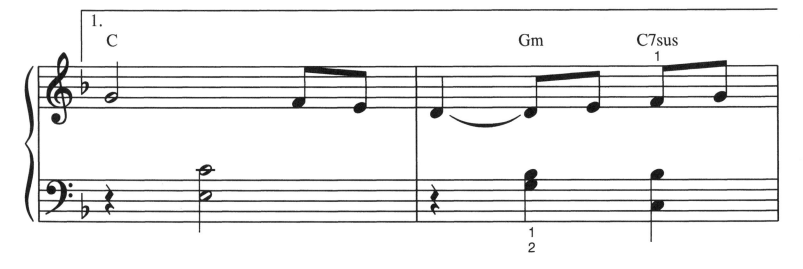

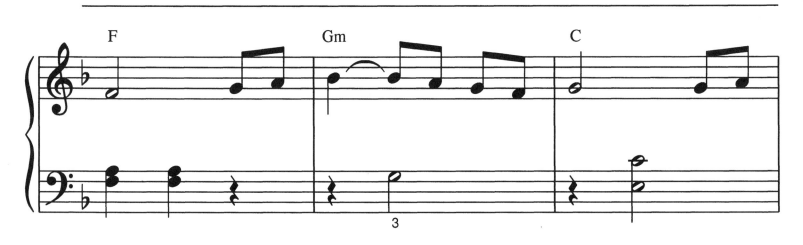

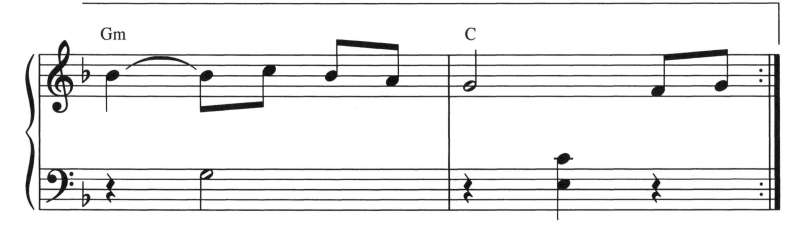

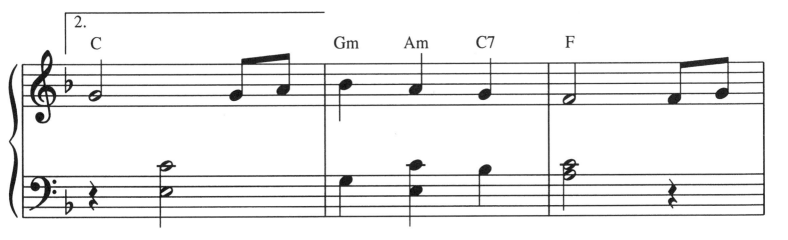

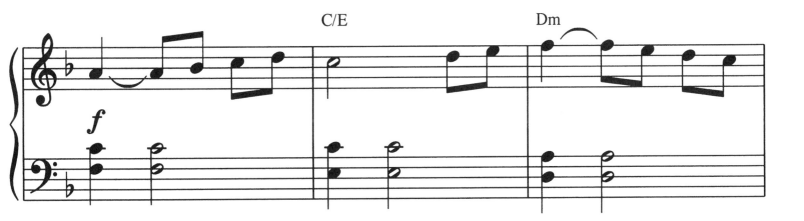

I HEARD THE BELLS ON CHRISTMAS DAY

Words by HENRY LONGFELLOW
Adapted by JOHNNY MARKS
Music by JOHNNY MARKS

Slowly

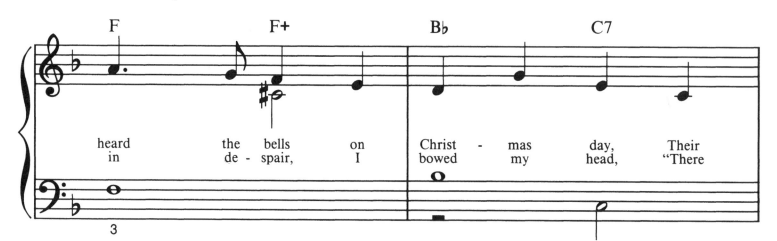

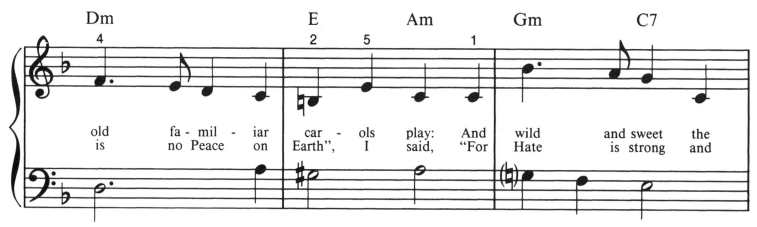

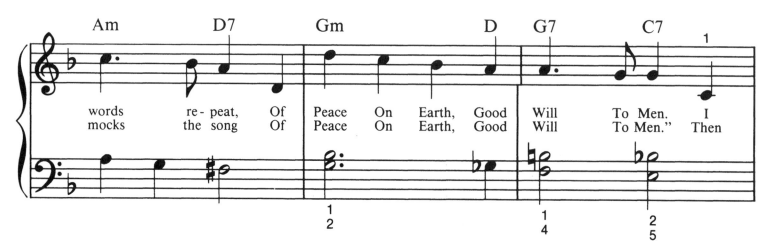

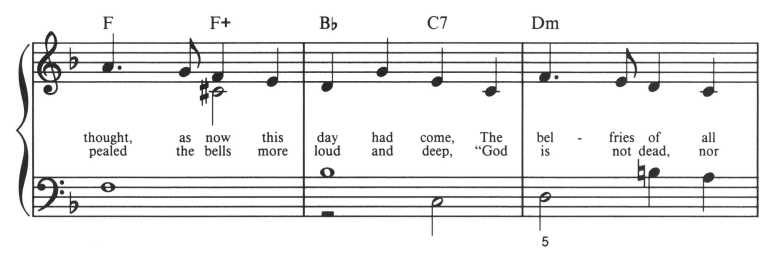

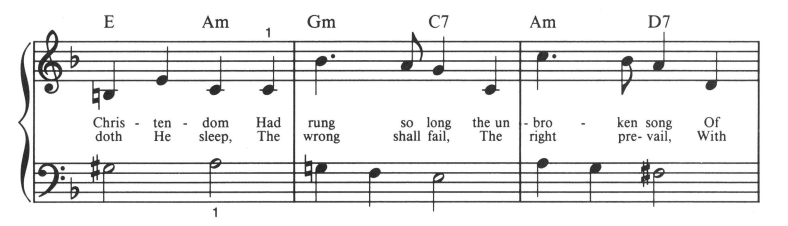

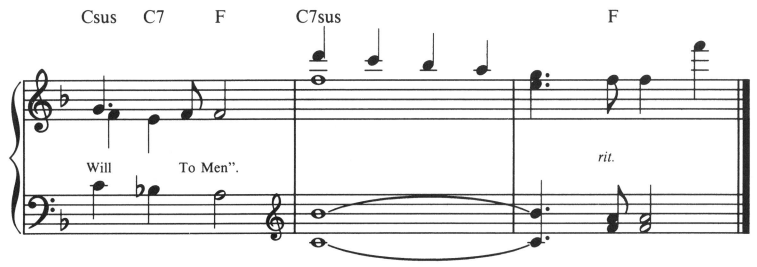

I SAW MOMMY
KISSING SANTA CLAUS

Words and Music by
TOMMIE CONNOR

Moderately Slow

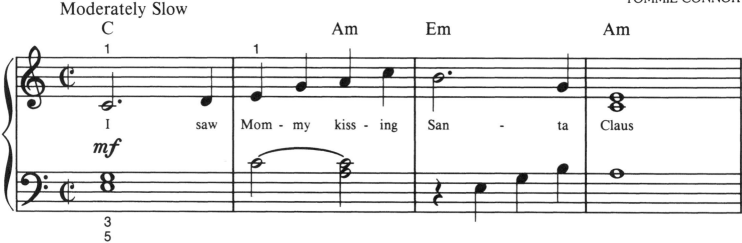

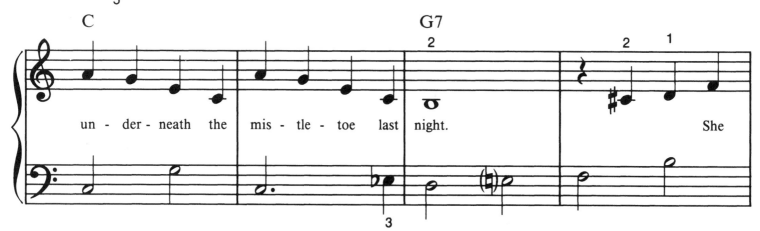

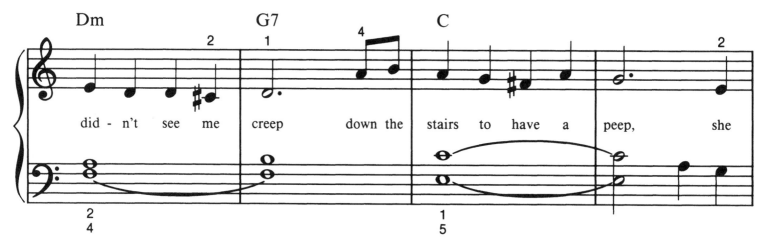

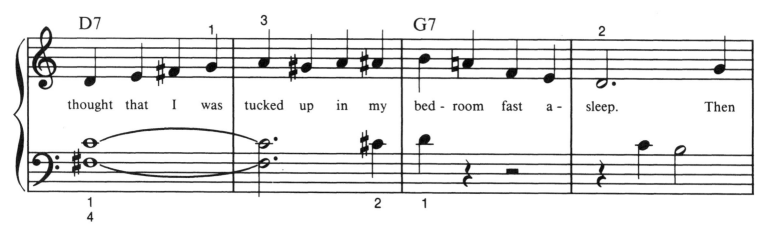

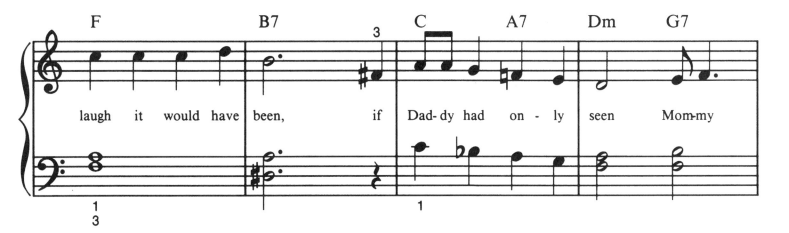

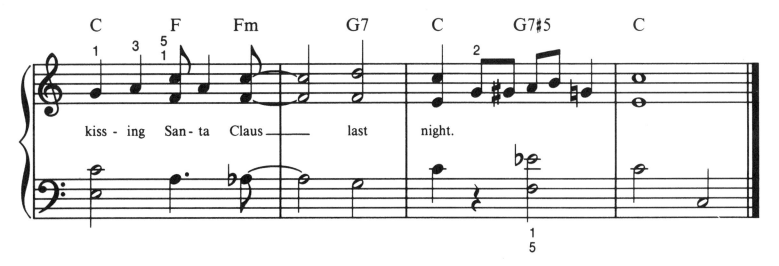

I SAW THREE SHIPS

Traditional English Carol

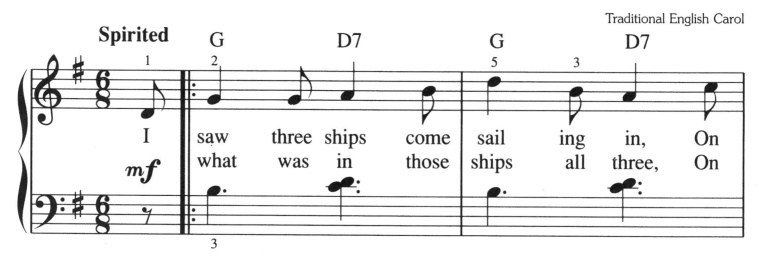

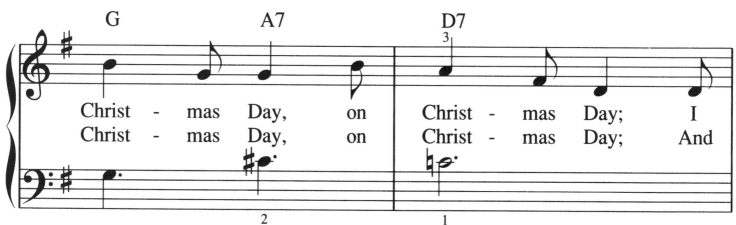

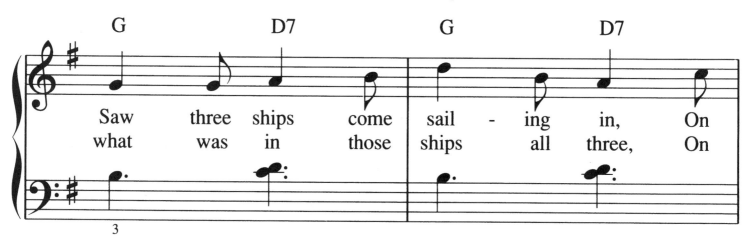

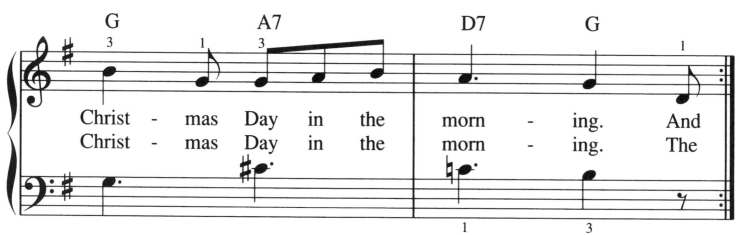

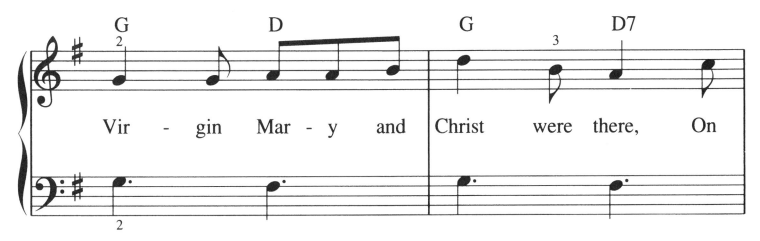

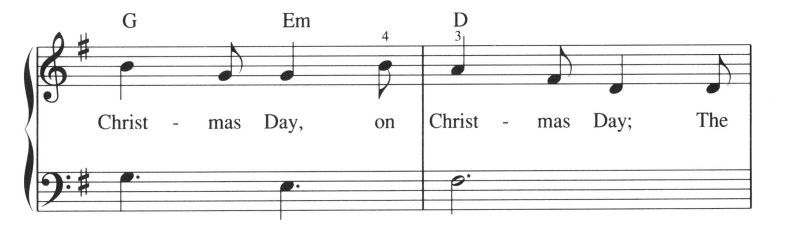

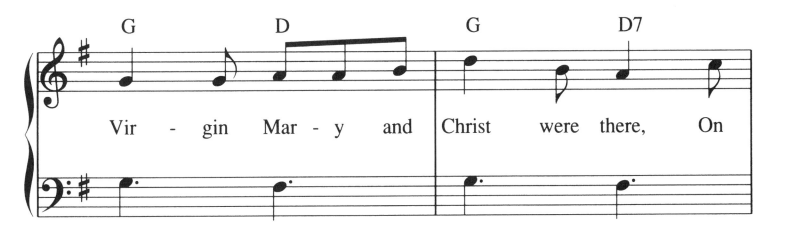

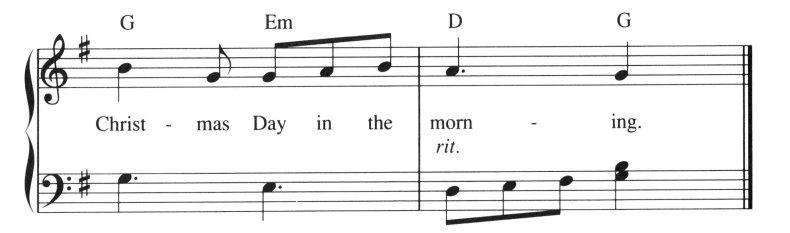

I'LL BE HOME FOR CHRISTMAS

Words and Music by KIM GANNON
and WALTER KENT

Slowly

mf legato

with pedal

C   Cdim

I'll   be   home   for

Dm   G7   Am

Christ - mas   You   can

A7♭9   Dm

plan   on   me.

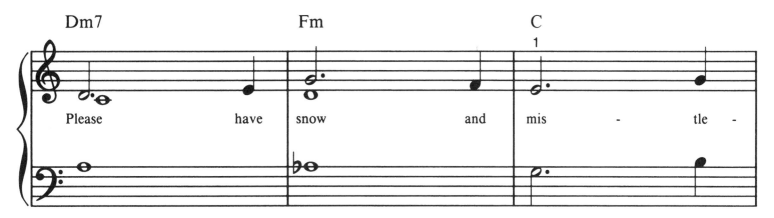

Dm7   Fm   C

Please   have snow   and   mis - tle -

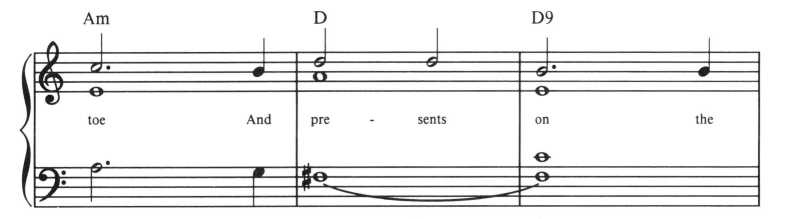

Am   D   D9

toe   And   pre - sents   on   the

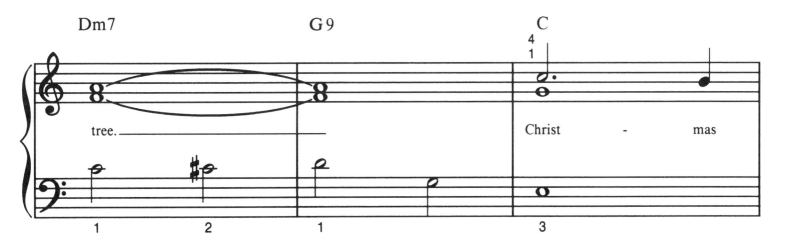

Dm7   G9   C

tree. _____   Christ - mas

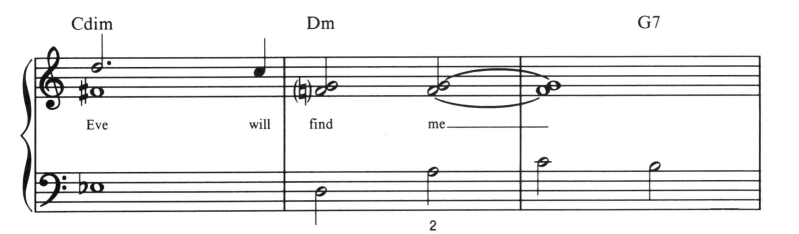

Cdim   Dm   G7

Eve   will find   me _____

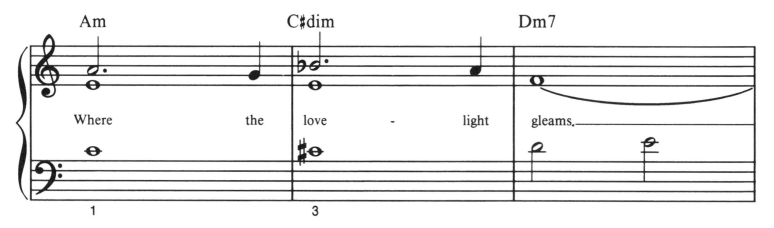

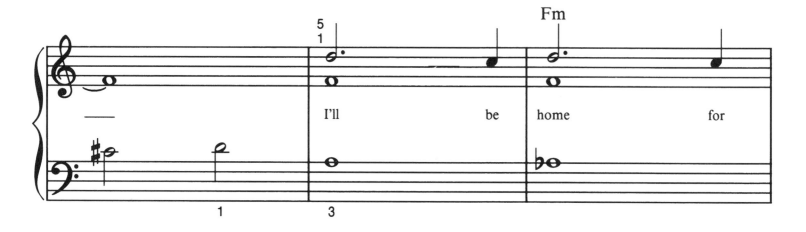

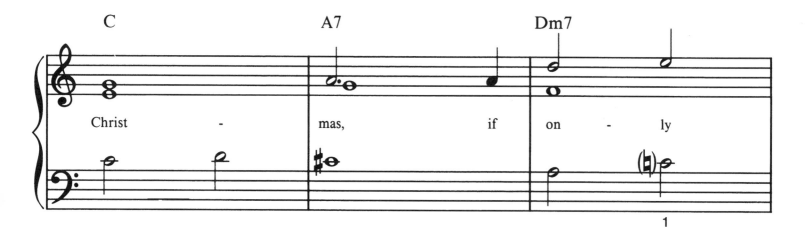

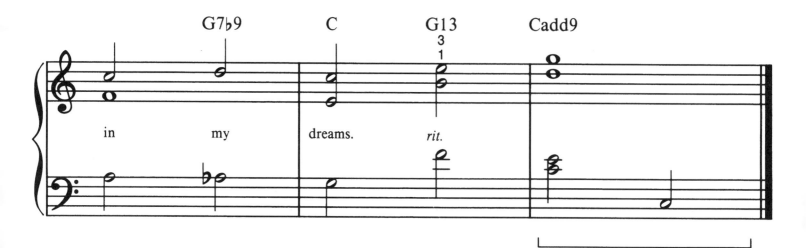

IT'S BEGINNING TO LOOK LIKE CHRISTMAS

Words and Music by
MEREDITH WILLSON

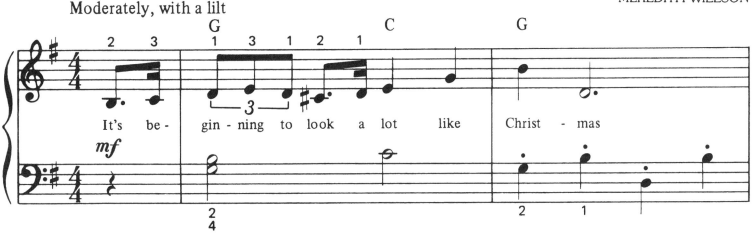

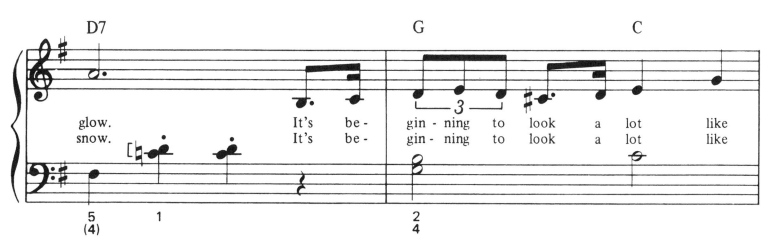

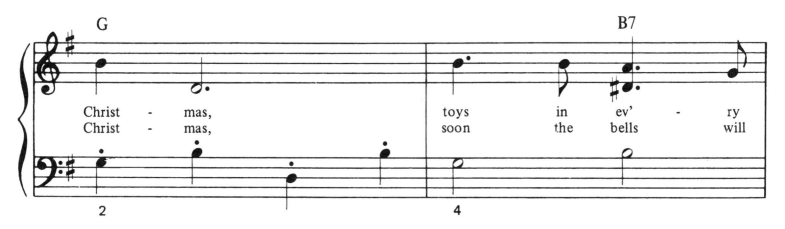

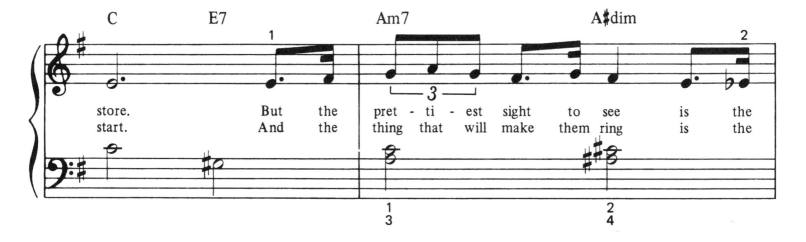

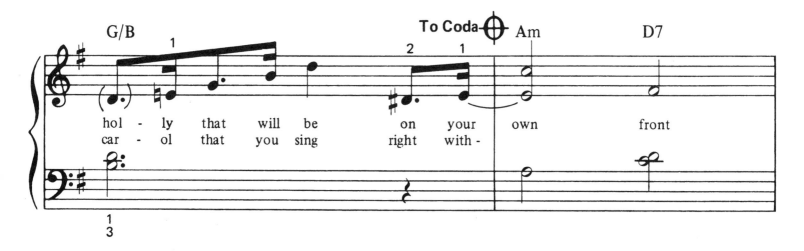

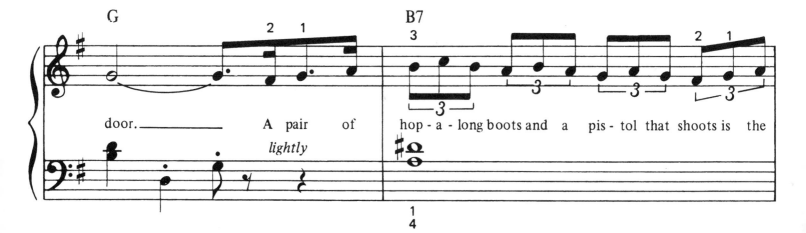

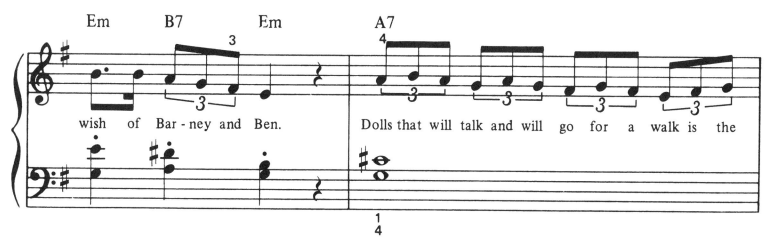

wish of Bar - ney and Ben. Dolls that will talk and will go for a walk is the

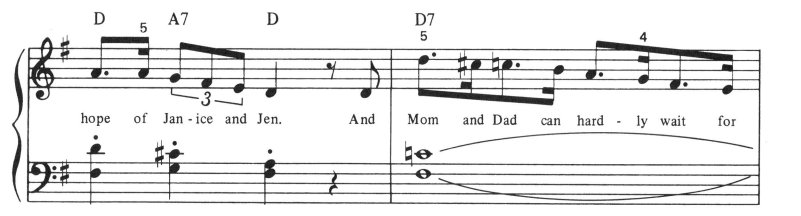

hope of Jan - ice and Jen. And Mom and Dad can hard - ly wait for

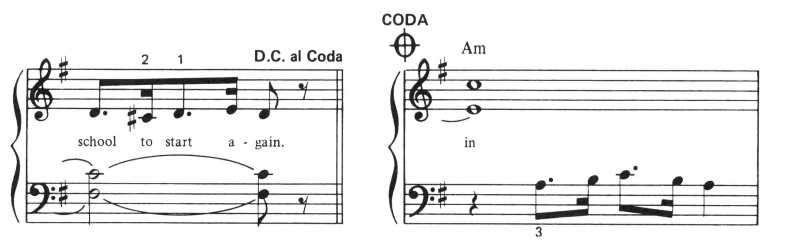

school to start a - gain. in

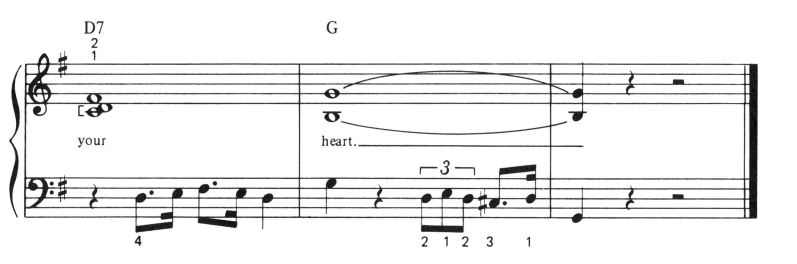

your heart.

INFANT HOLY, INFANT LOWLY

Traditional Polish Carol

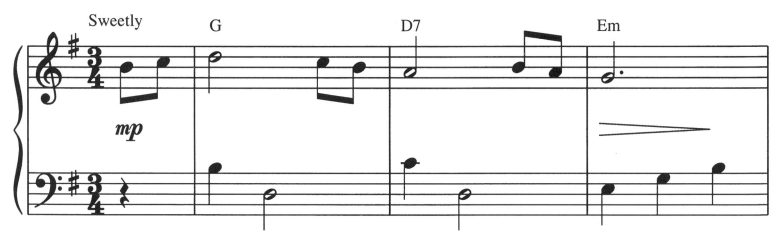

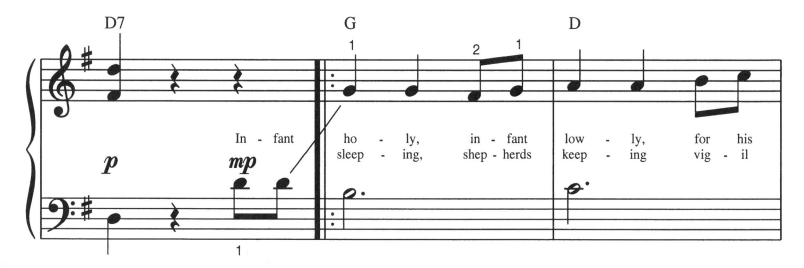

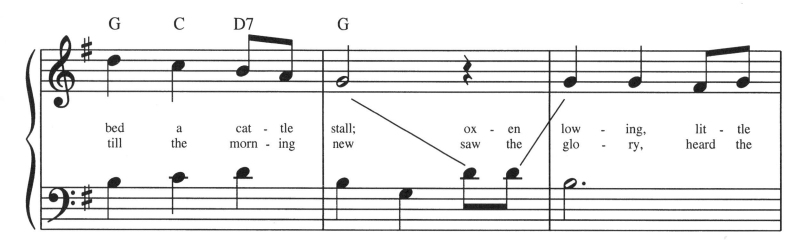

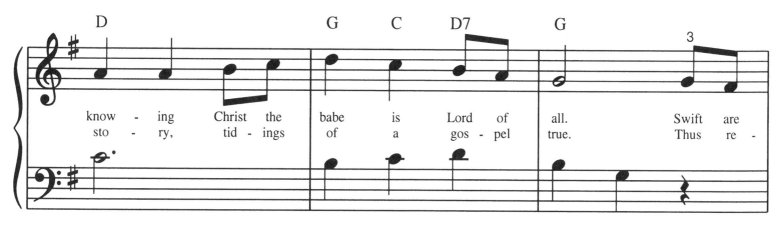

know - ing Christ the babe is Lord of all. Swift are
sto - ry, tid - ings of a gos - pel true. Thus re -

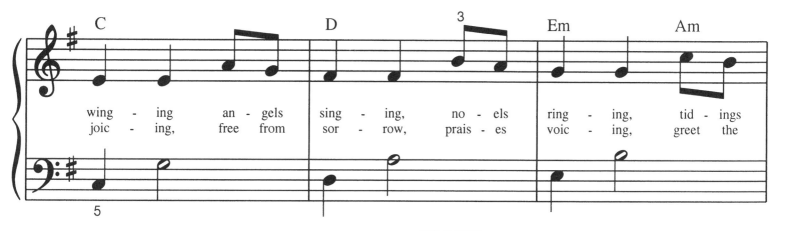

wing - ing an - gels sing - ing, no - els ring - ing, tid - ings
joic - ing, free from sor - row, prais - es voic - ing, greet the

bring - ing: Christ the Babe is Lord of all.
mor - row: Christ the Babe was born for you.

p

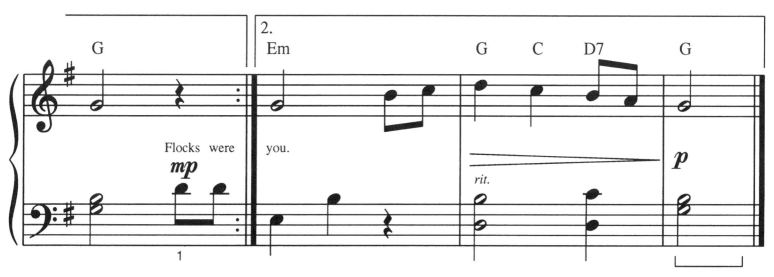

Flocks were you.
mp
rit.
p

IT CAME UPON
THE MIDNIGHT CLEAR

Words by EDMUND H. SEARS
Music by RICHARD STORRS WILLIS

Gently

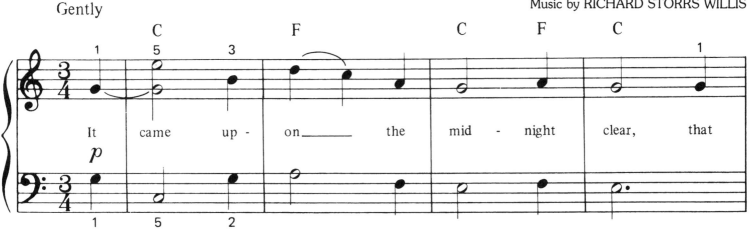

It came up - on ____ the mid - night clear, that

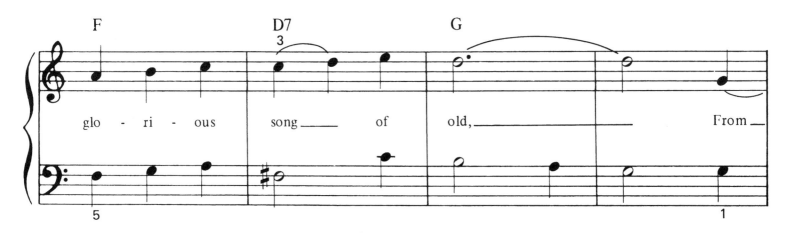

glo - ri - ous song ____ of old, _____ From ____

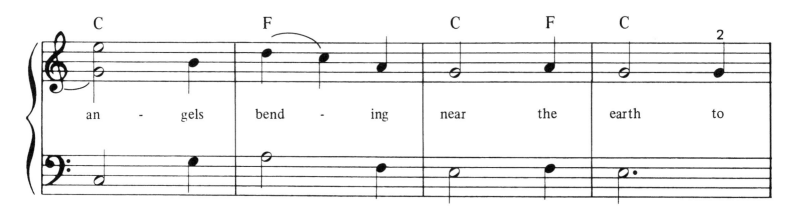

an - gels bend - ing near the earth to

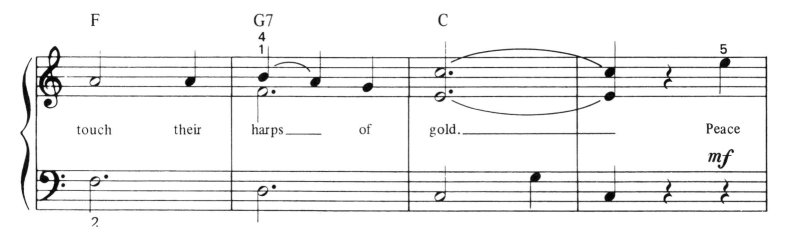

touch their harps ____ of gold. _____ Peace

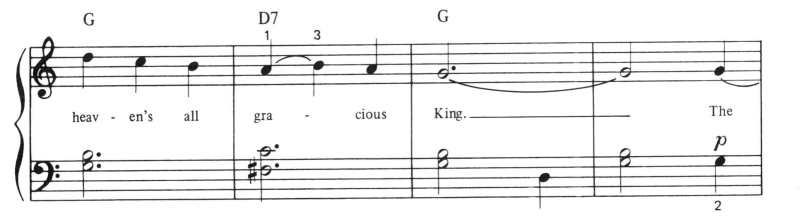

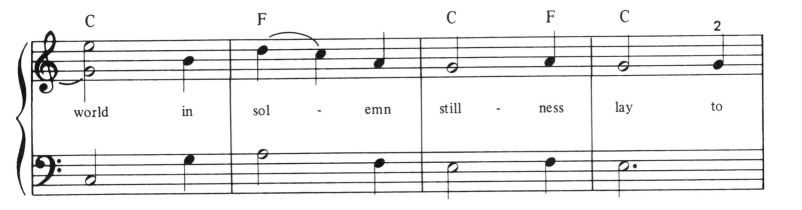

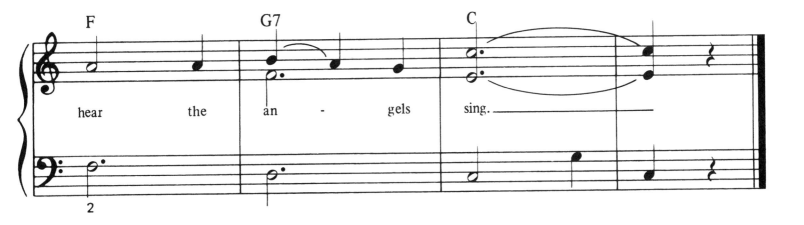

JINGLE-BELL ROCK

Words and Music by JOE BEAL
and JIM BOOTHE

Moderately

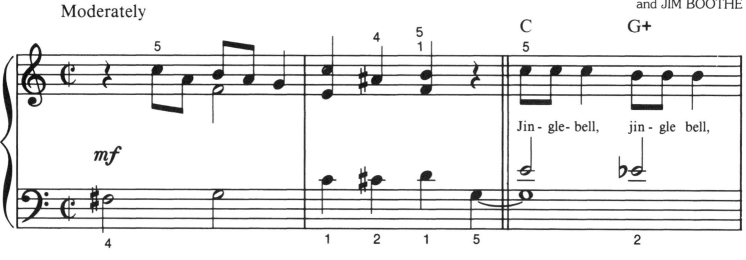

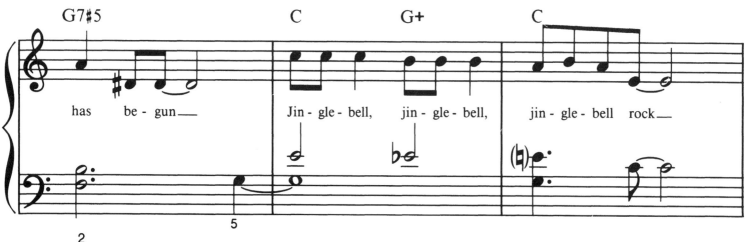

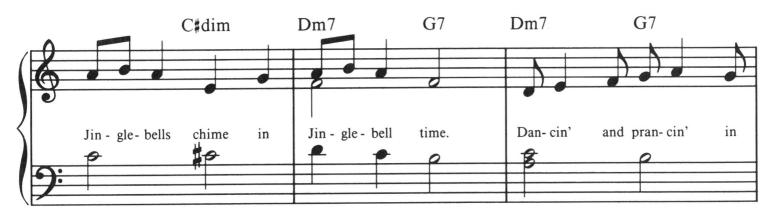

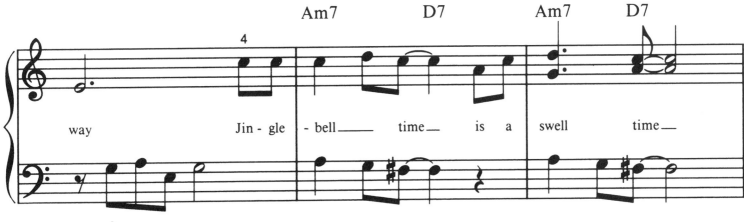

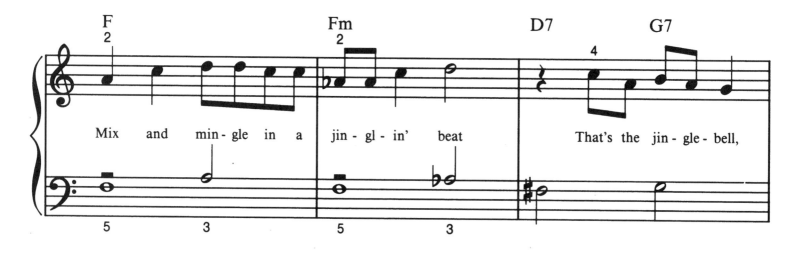

JINGLE BELLS

Words and Music by
J. PIERPONT

Moderately

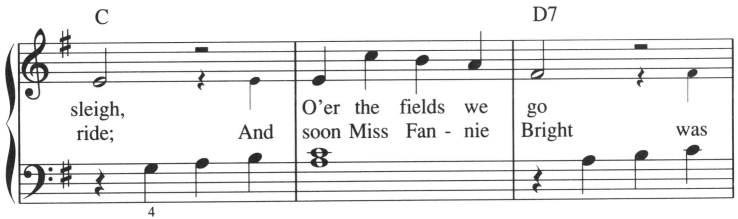

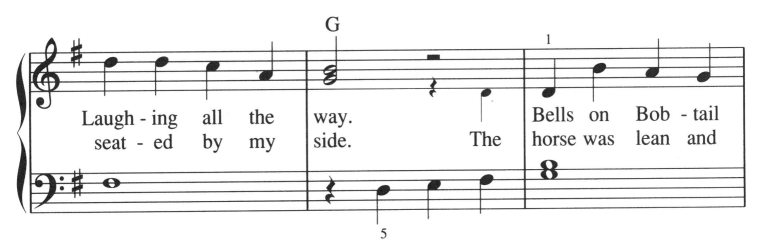

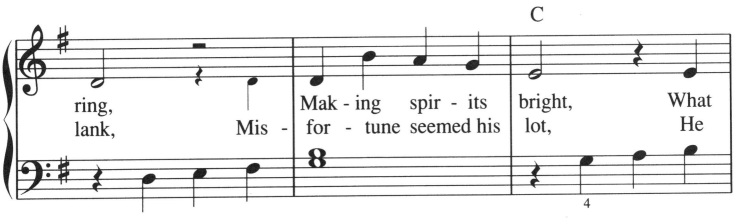

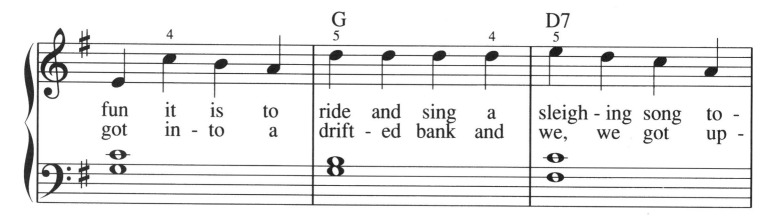

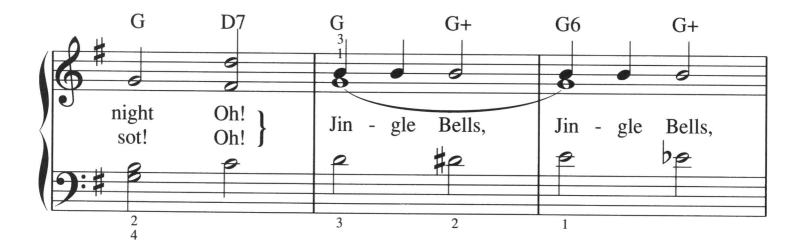

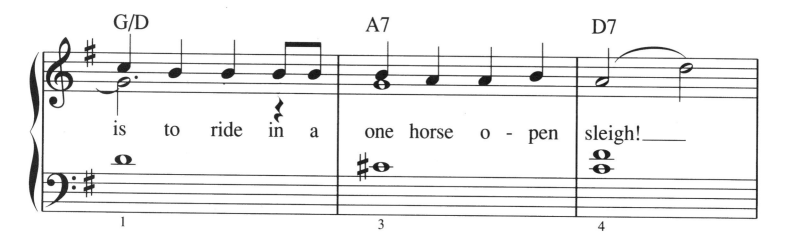

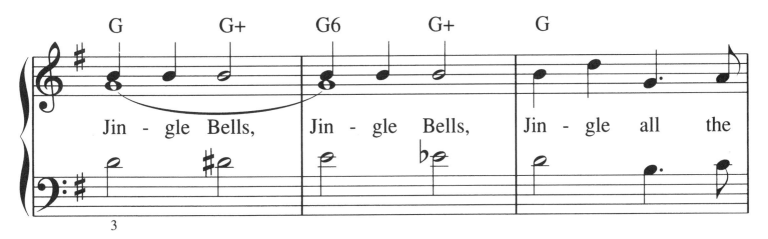

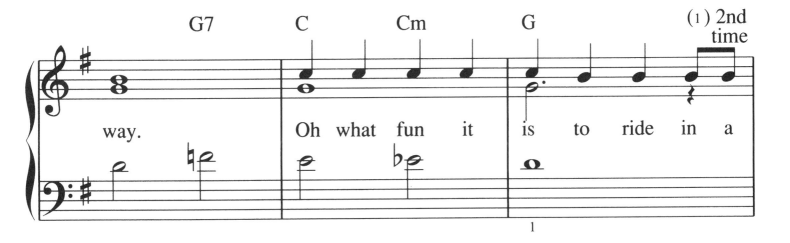

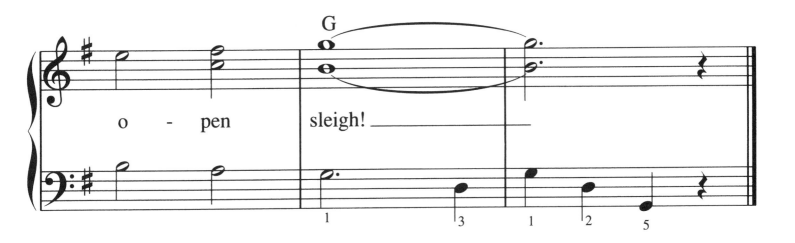

JOLLY OLD ST. NICHOLAS

Traditional 19th Century American Carol

Brightly

G   D/F#

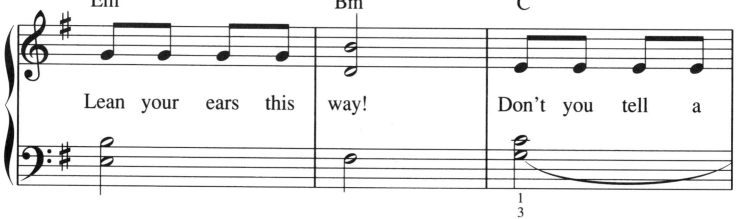

Jol - ly old Saint Ni - cho - las,

Em   Bm   C

Lean your ears this way! Don't you tell a

G   D7

sin - gle soul! What I'm going to say;

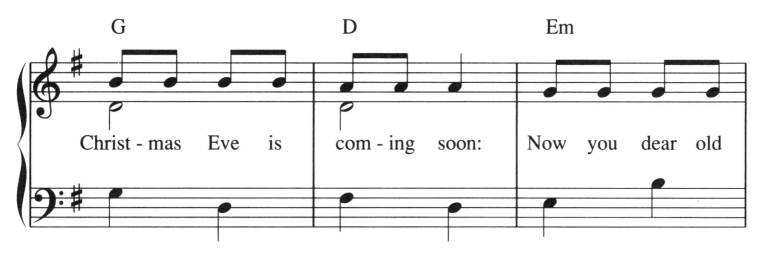

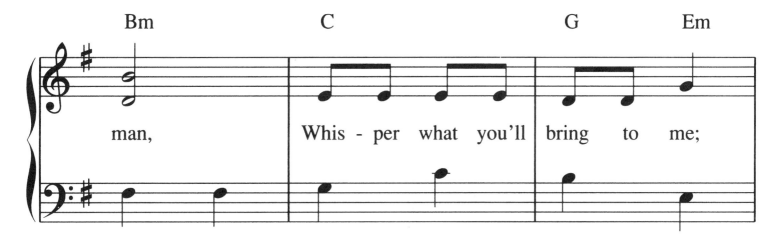

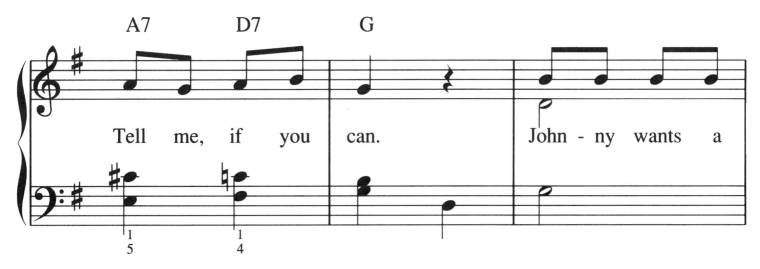

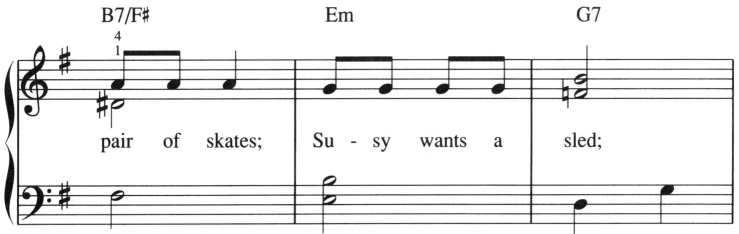

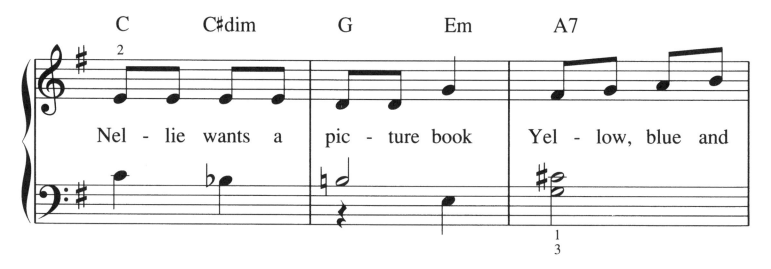

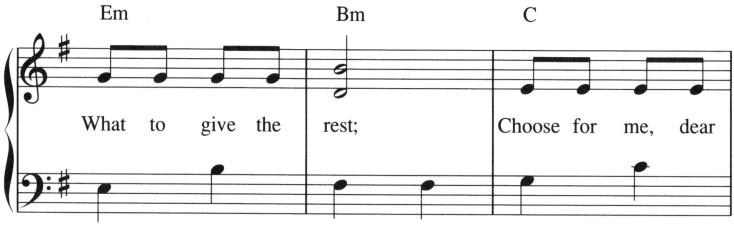

LET IT SNOW! LET IT SNOW! LET IT SNOW!

Words by SAMMY CAHN
Music by JULE STYNE

Moderately

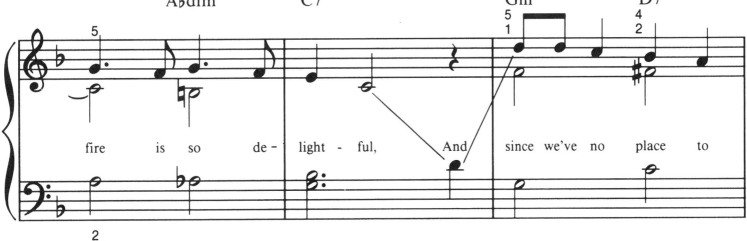

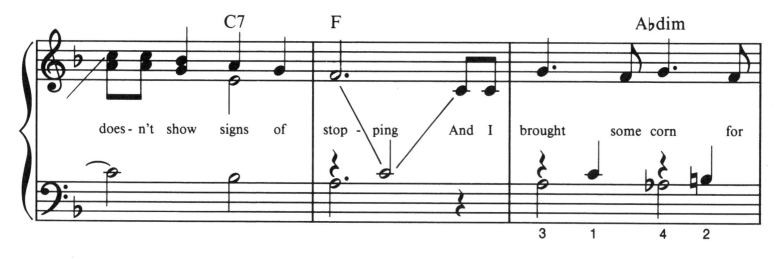

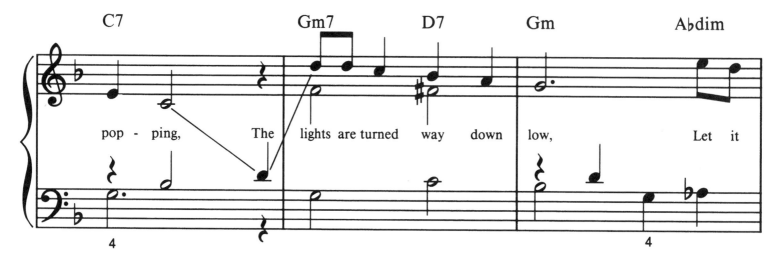

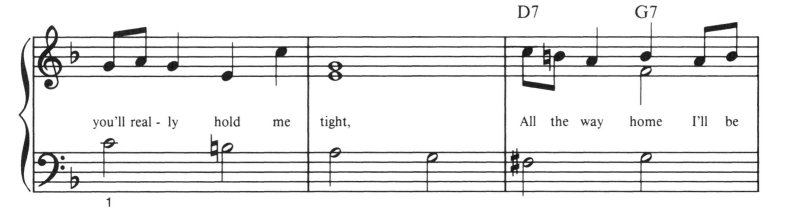

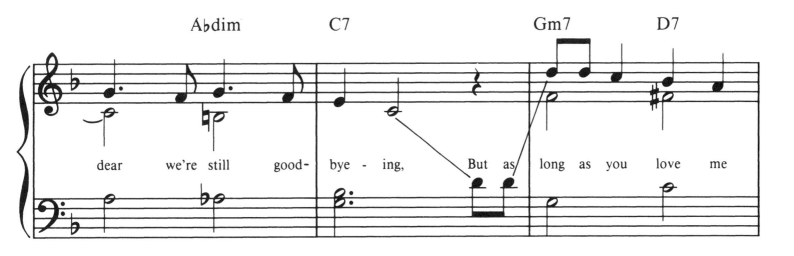

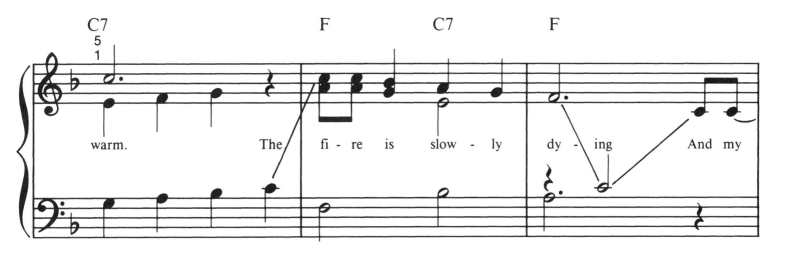

JOY TO THE WORLD

Words by ISAAC WATTS
Music by GEORGE F. HANDEL

Moderately

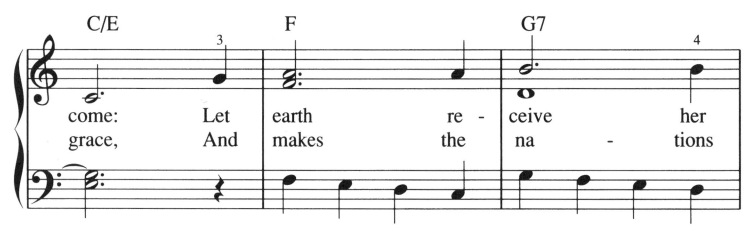

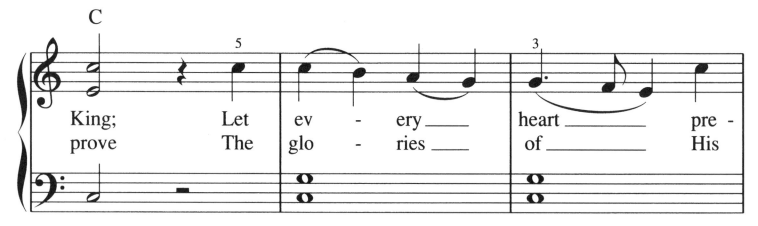

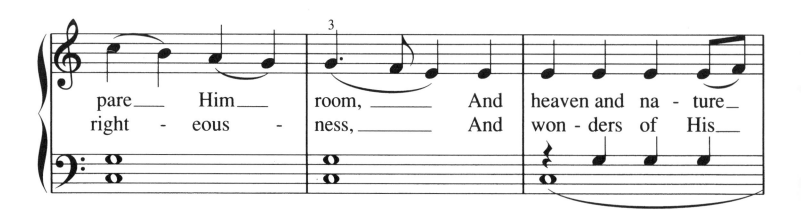

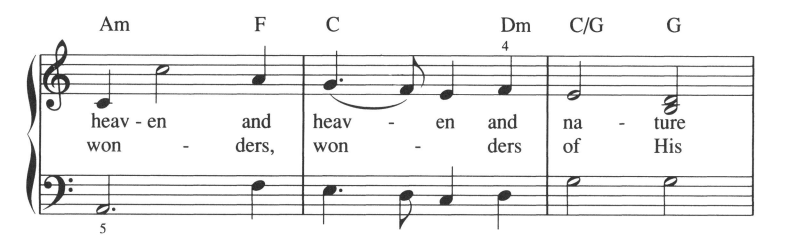

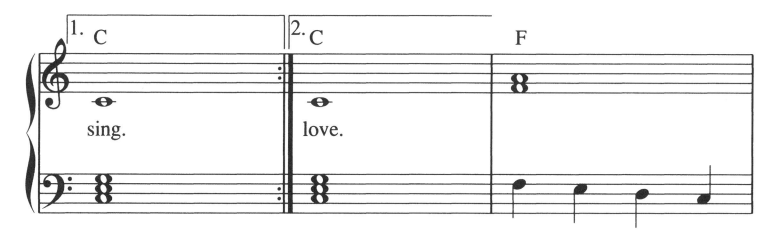

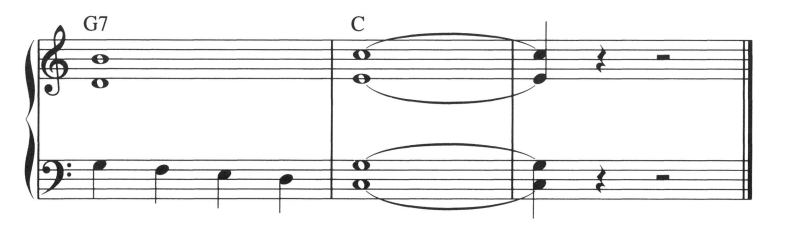

LO, HOW A ROSE E'ER BLOOMING
from the ALTE CATHOLISCHE GEISTLICHE KIRCHENGESANG

Slowly

15th Century German Tune

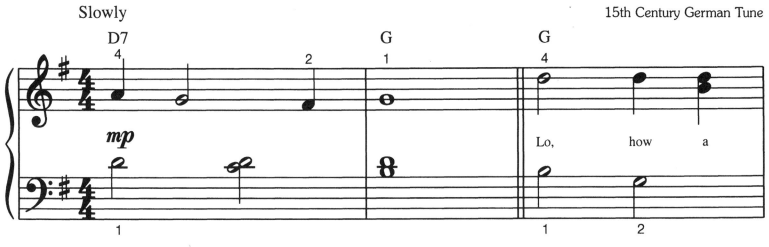

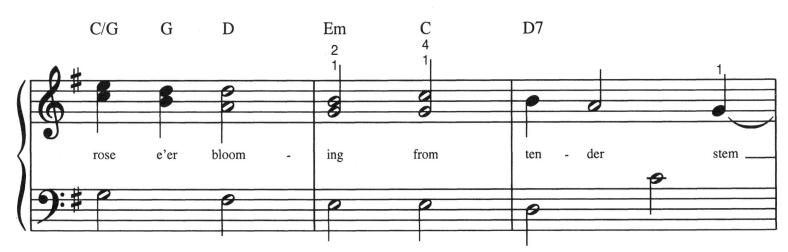

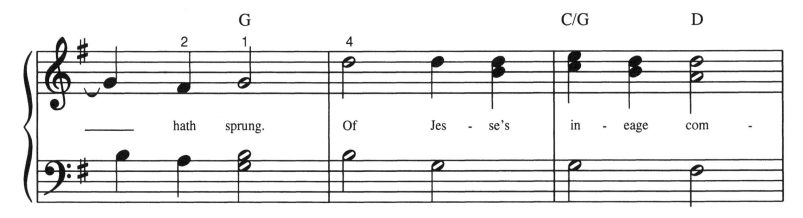

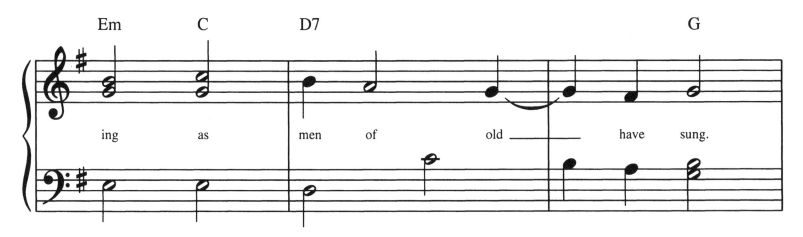

105

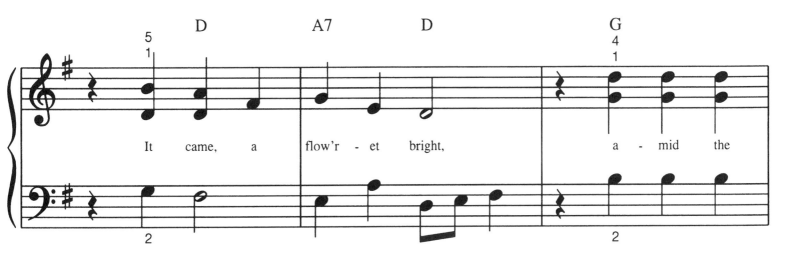

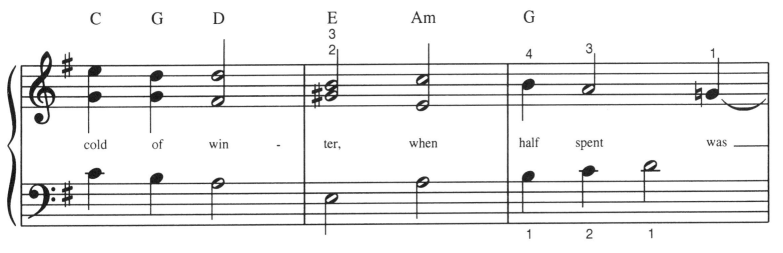

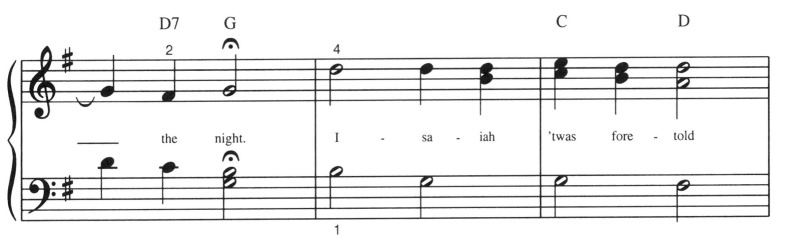

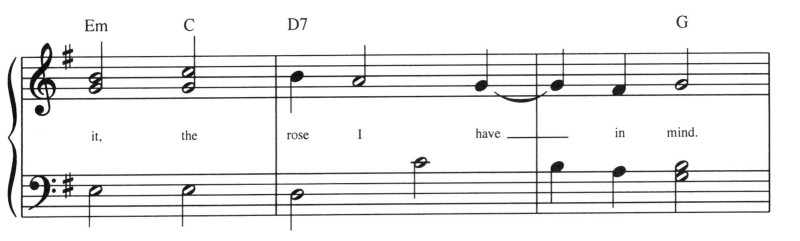

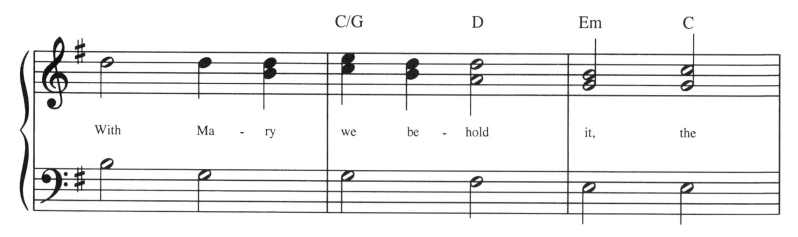

With   Ma - ry   we   be - hold   it,   the

Vir - gin   Moth - er   kind.   To   show   God's

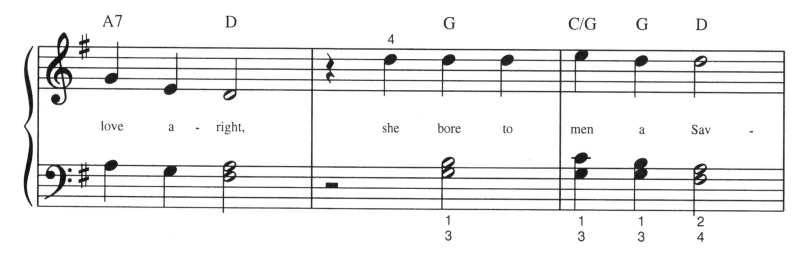

love   a - right,   she   bore   to   men   a   Sav -

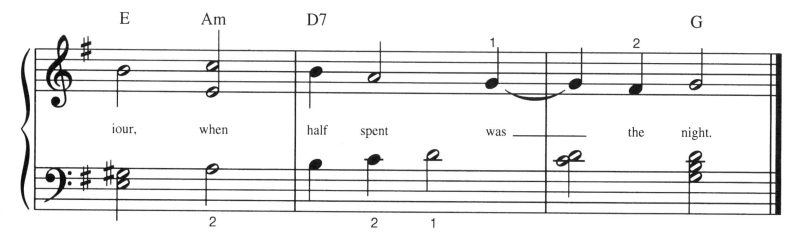

iour,   when   half   spent   was ____   the   night.

O CHRISTMAS TREE

Traditional German Carol

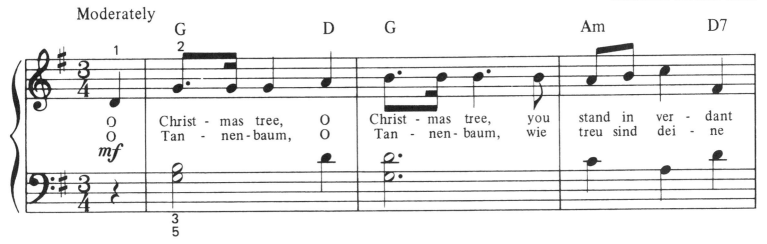

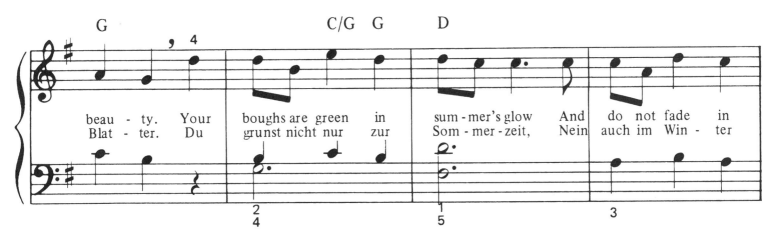

MARY HAD A BABY

African-American Spiritual

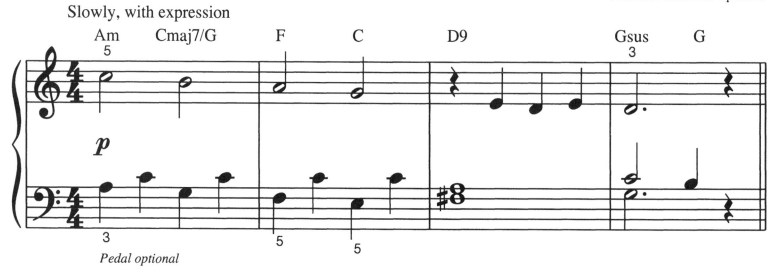

Slowly, with expression

Pedal optional

Ma - ry had a ba - by, my Lord.
Laid him in a man - ger, my Lord,

Ma - ry had a ba - by,
laid him in a man - ger,

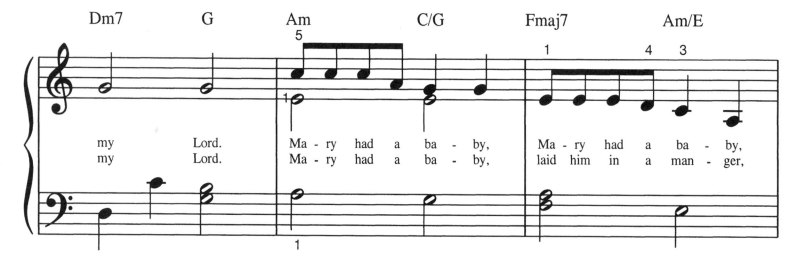

my Lord.
my Lord.

Ma - ry had a ba - by,
Ma - ry had a ba - by,

Ma - ry had a ba - by,
laid him in a man - ger,

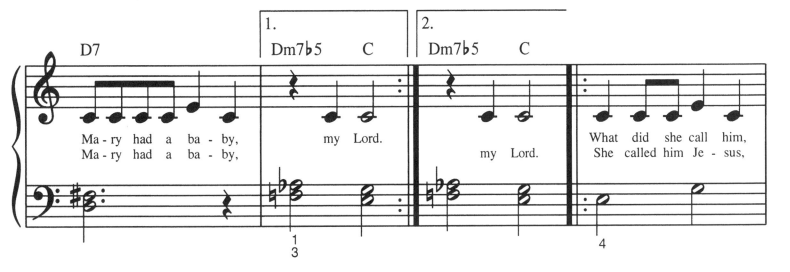

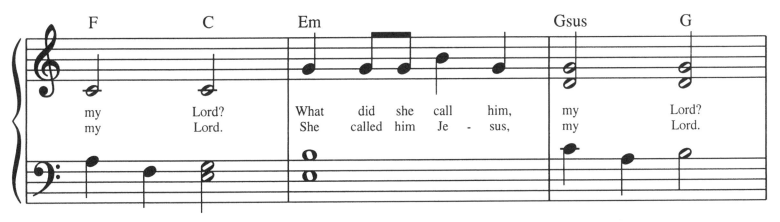

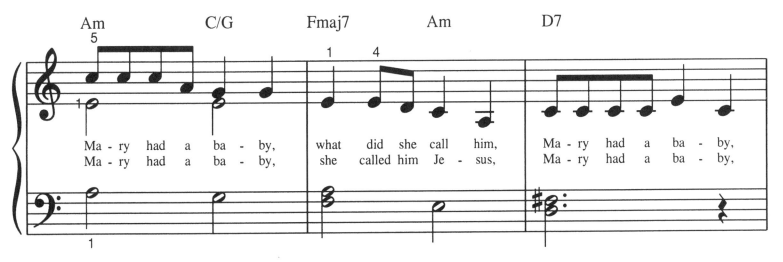

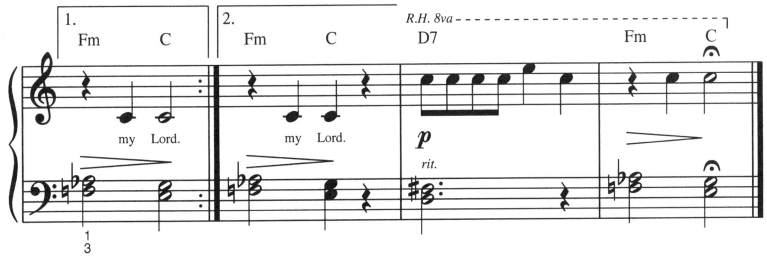

MISTER SANTA

Words and Music by
PAT BALLARD

Brightly, in 2 (♩ = 1 beat)

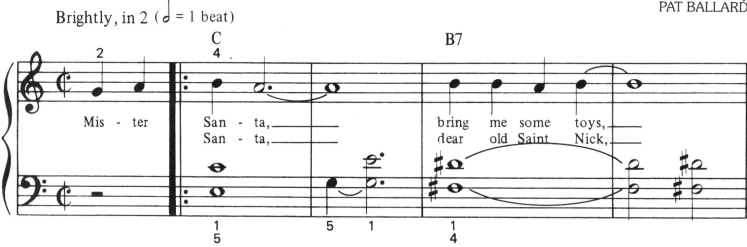

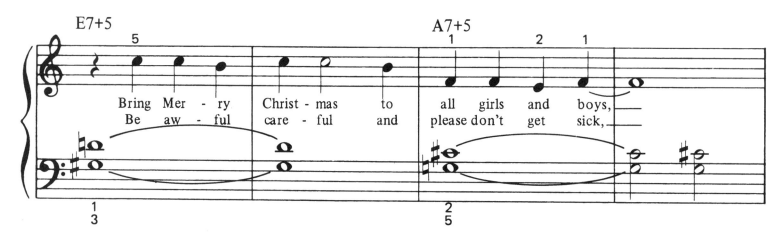

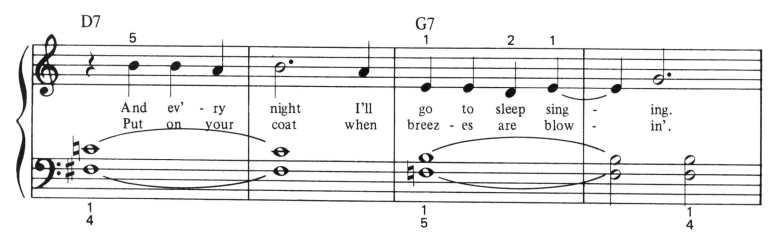

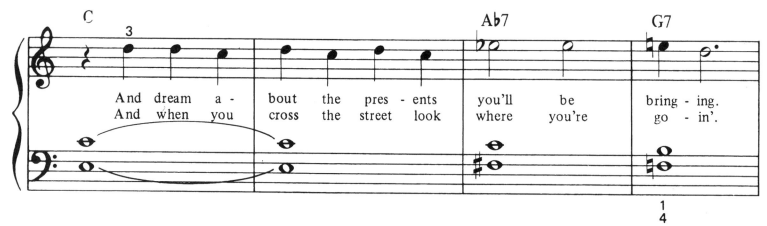

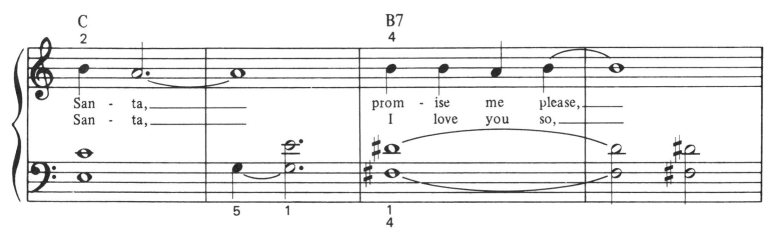

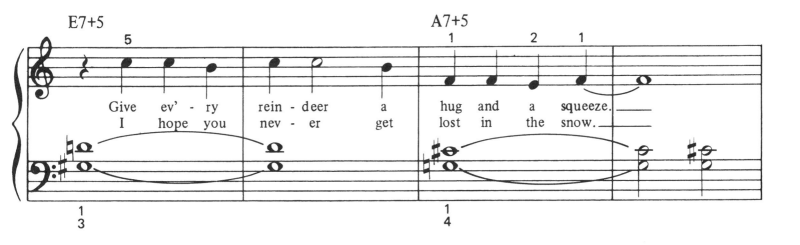

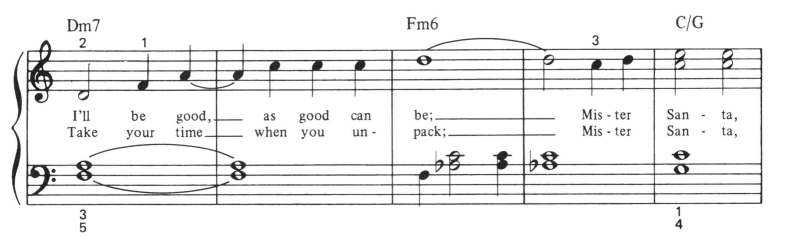

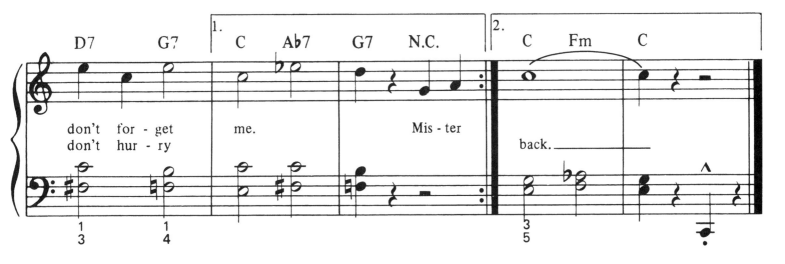

THE MOST WONDERFUL TIME OF THE YEAR

Words and Music by EDDIE POLA
and GEORGE WYLE

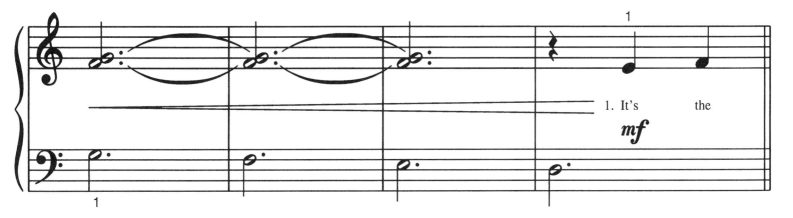

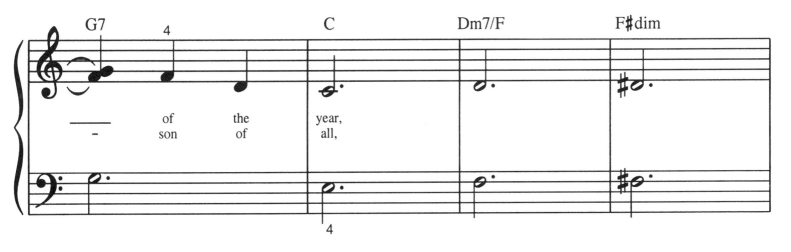

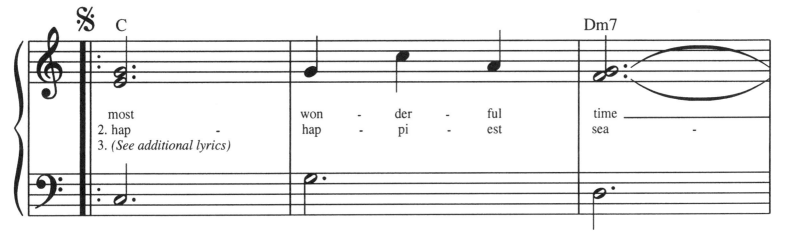

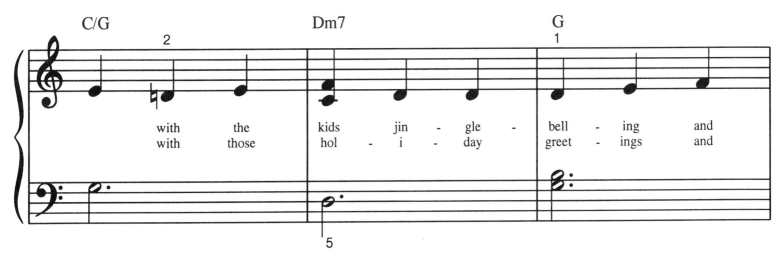

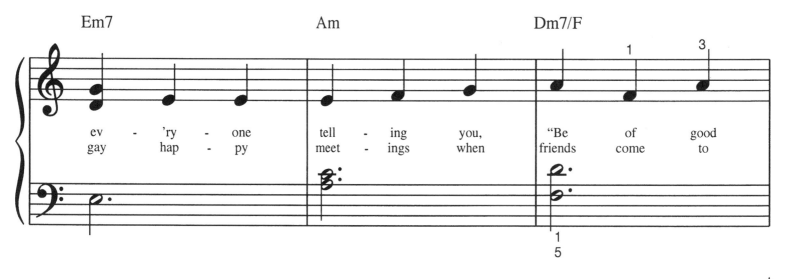

Em7   Am   Dm7/F

ev - 'ry - one   tell - ing   you,   "Be   of   good
gay   hap - py   meet - ings   when   friends   come   to

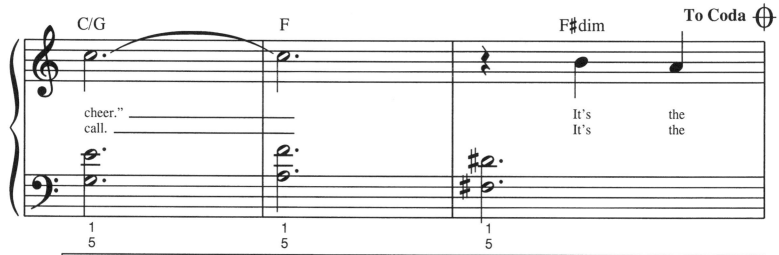

C/G   F   F#dim   **To Coda** ⊕

cheer." _____
call. _____

It's   the
It's   the

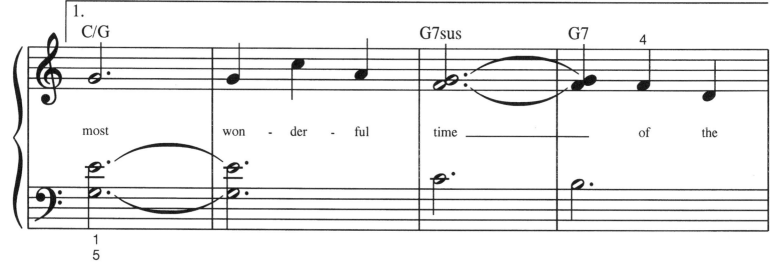

1.
C/G   G7sus   G7

most   won - der - ful   time _____   of   the

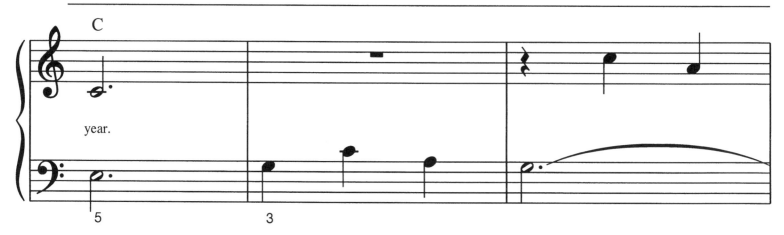

C

year.

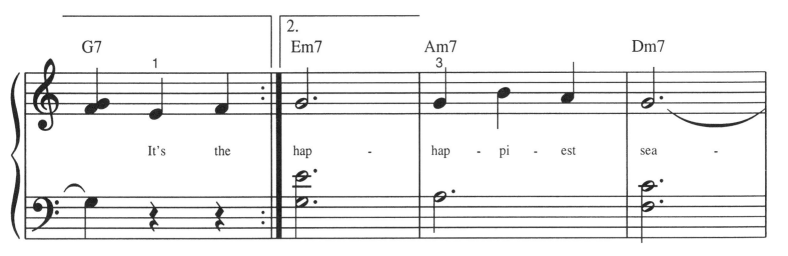

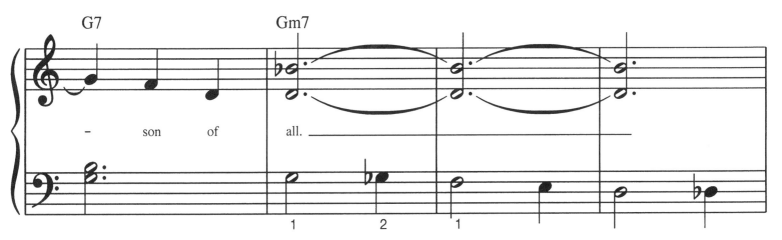

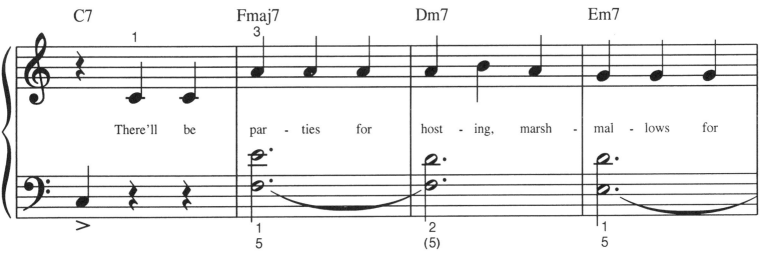

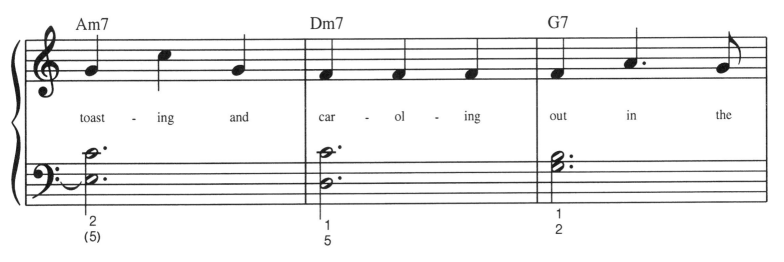

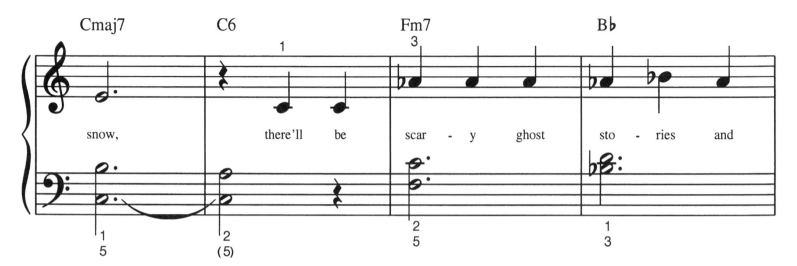

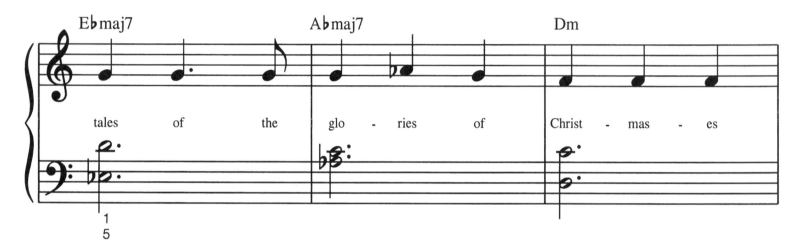

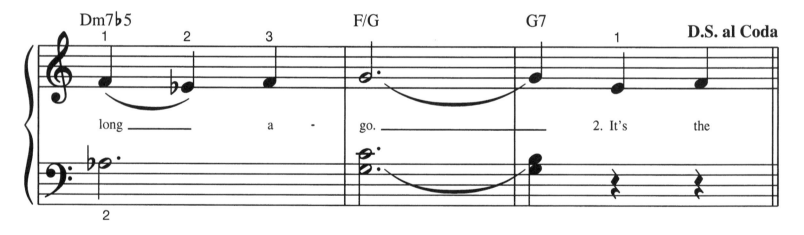

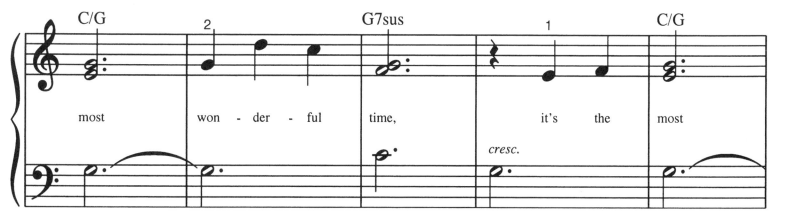

most wonーderーful time, it's the most

cresc.

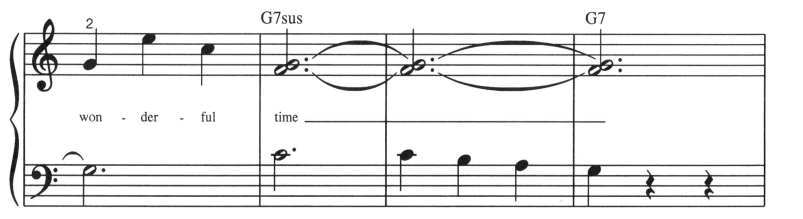

wonーderーful time

of the year.

f

sfz

8va

8vb

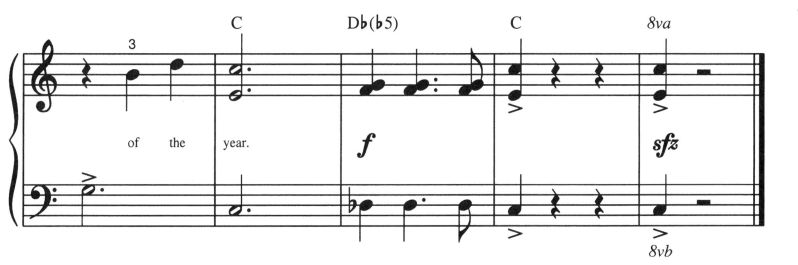

Additional Lyrics

3. It's the most wonderful time of the year.
There'll be much mistletoeing and hearts will be glowing
    when loved ones are near.
It's the most wonderful time,
It's the most wonderful time,
It's the most wonderful time of the year.

O COME, ALL YE FAITHFUL
(Adeste Fidelis)

Words and Music by JOHN FRANCIS WADE
Latin Words translated by FREDERICK OAKELEY

Moderately

O come, all ye faith - ful,

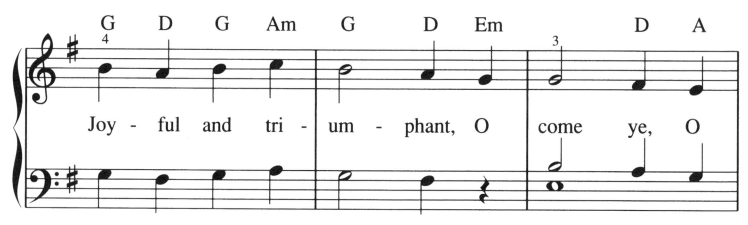

Joy - ful and tri - um - phant, O come ye, O

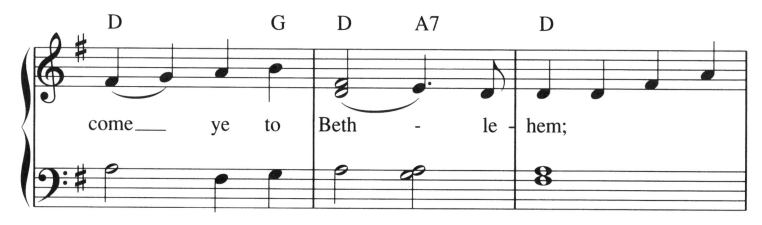

come ___ ye to Beth - le - hem;

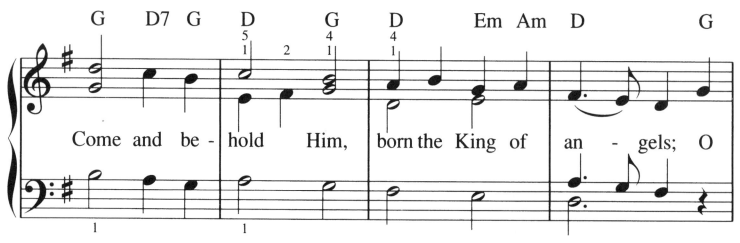

Come and be - hold Him, born the King of an - gels; O

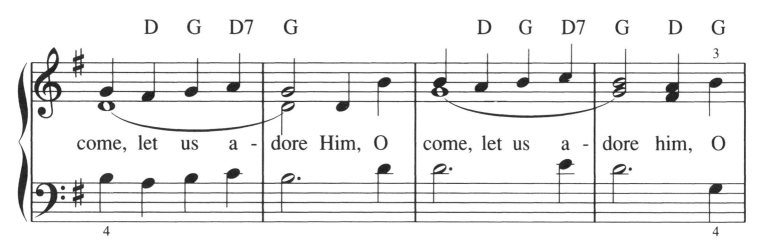

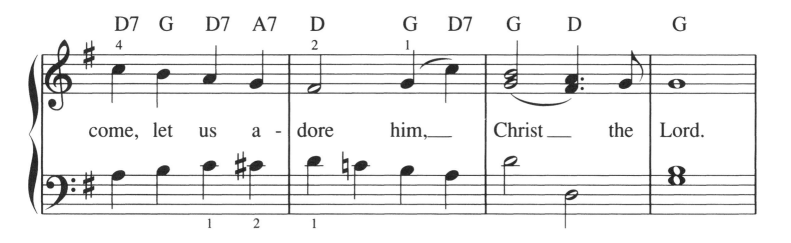

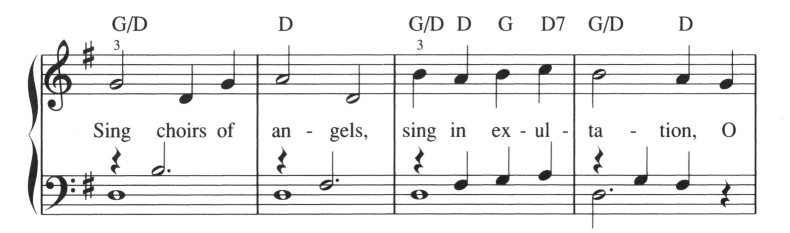

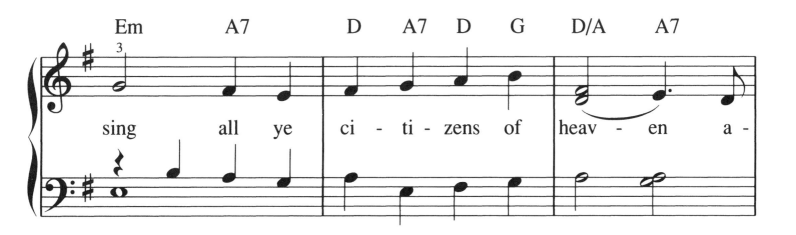

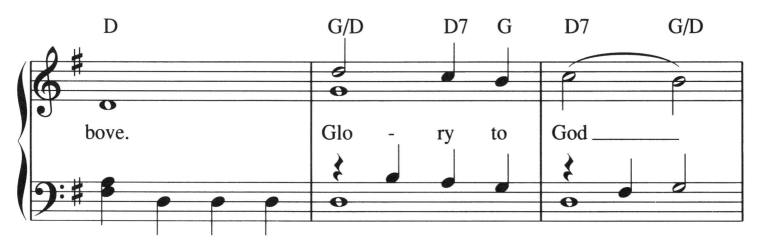

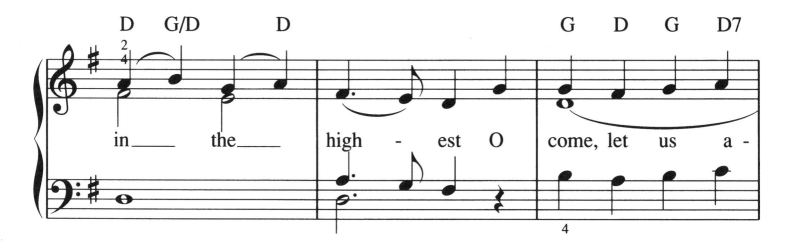

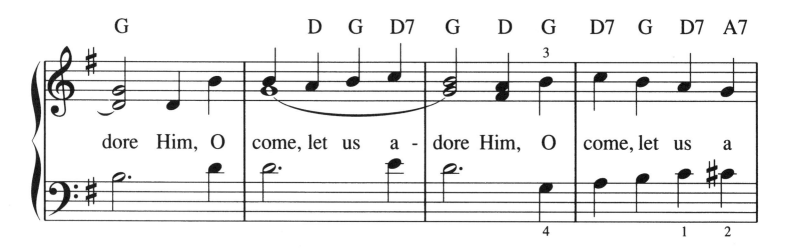

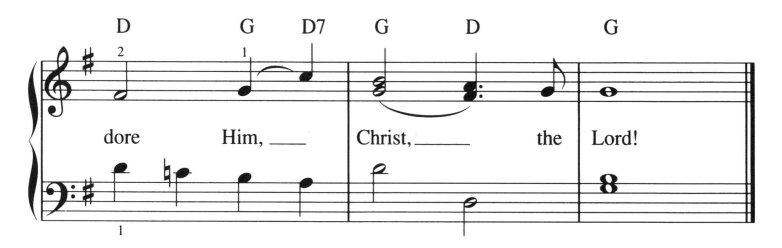

O HOLY NIGHT

French Words by PLACIDE CAPPEAU
English Words by D.S. DWIGHT
Music by ADOLPHE ADAM

Slow and Solemn (in 2, ♩ = 1 beat)

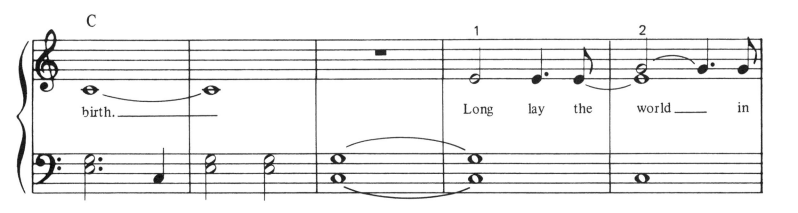

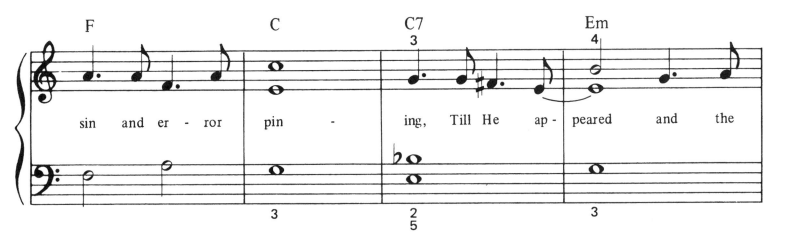

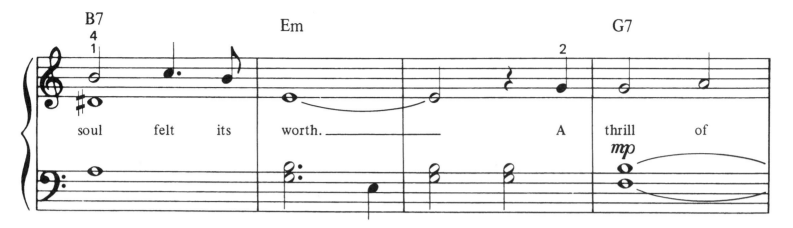

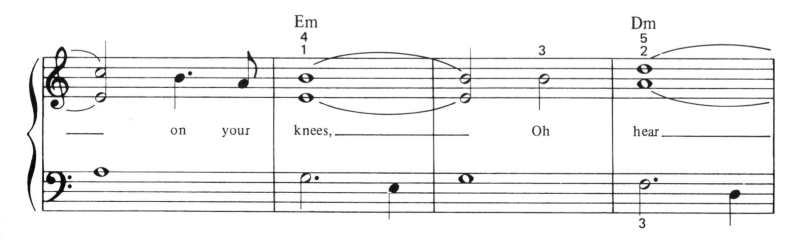

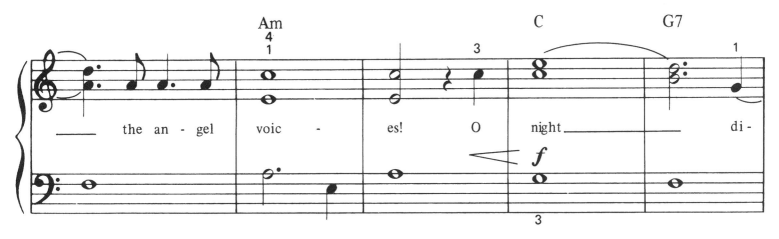

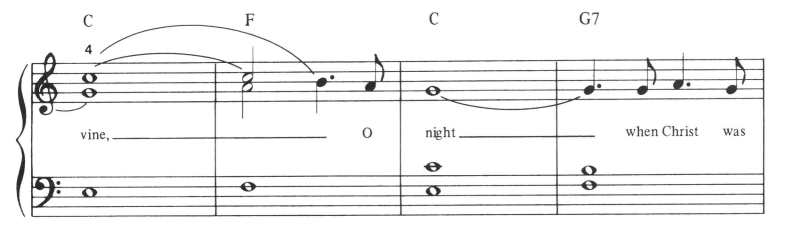

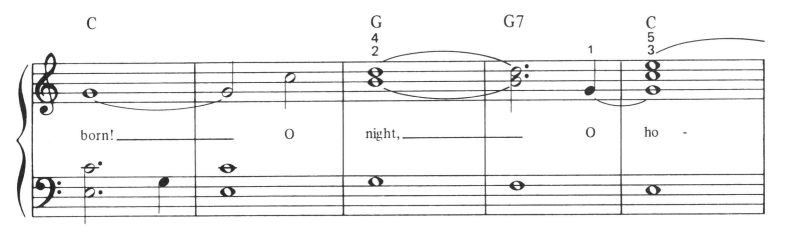

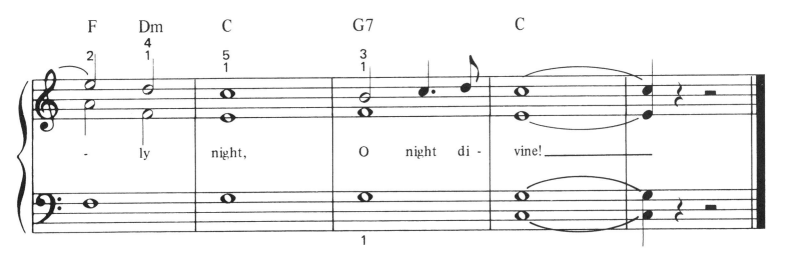

O LITTLE TOWN OF BETHLEHEM

Words by PHILLIPS BROOKS
Music by LEWIS H. REDNER

Moderately

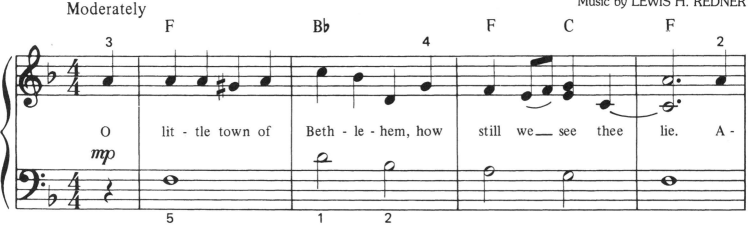

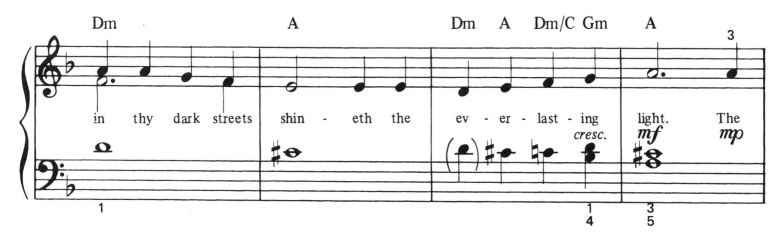

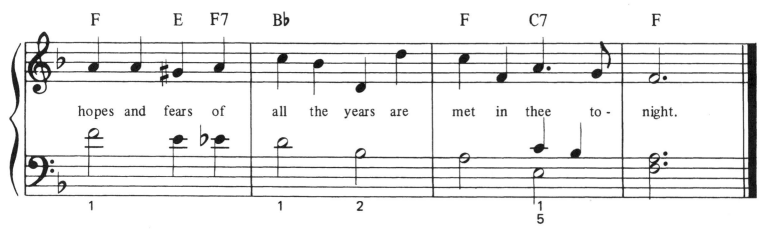

PLEASE COME HOME
FOR CHRISTMAS

Words and Music by CHARLES BROWN
and GENE REDD

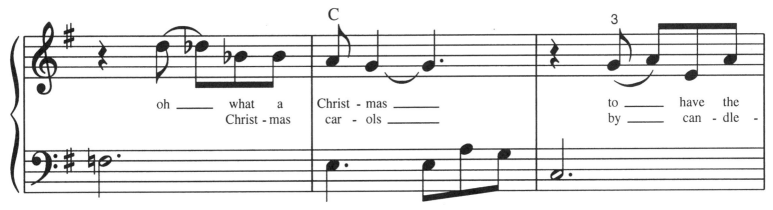

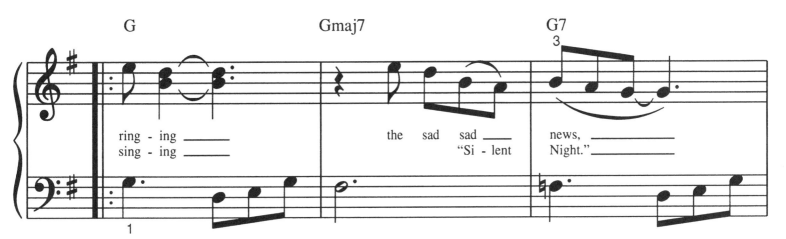

I have no friends _____ to wish me
Please come home for Christ - mas _____ if not me for

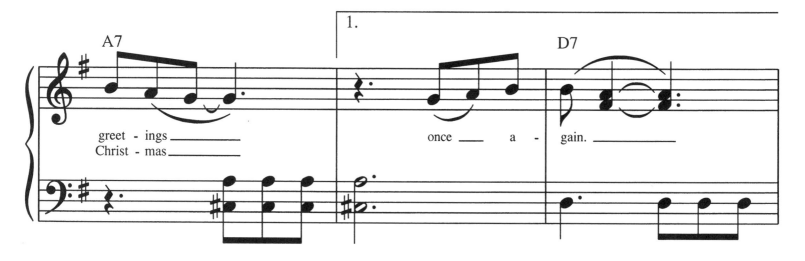

1.

greet - ings _____ once ____ a - gain. _____
Christ - mas _____

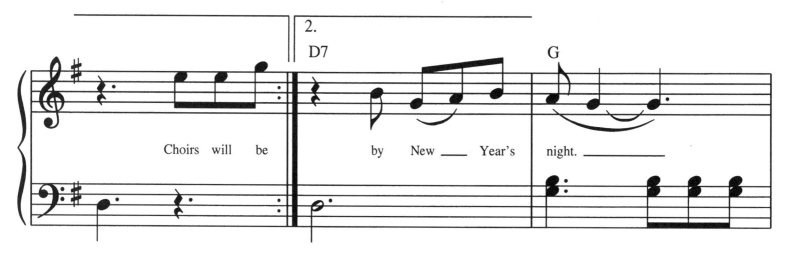

2.

Choirs will be by New ____ Year's night. _____

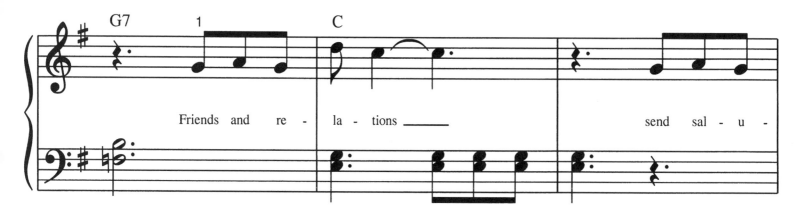

Friends and re - la - tions _____ send sal - u -

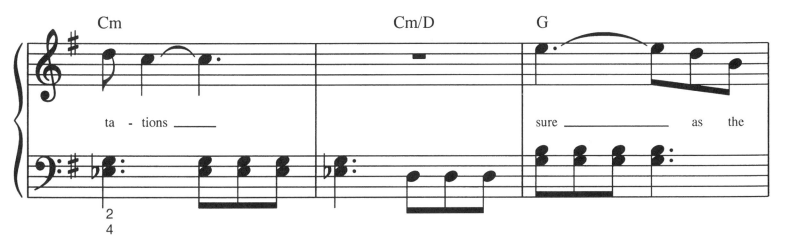

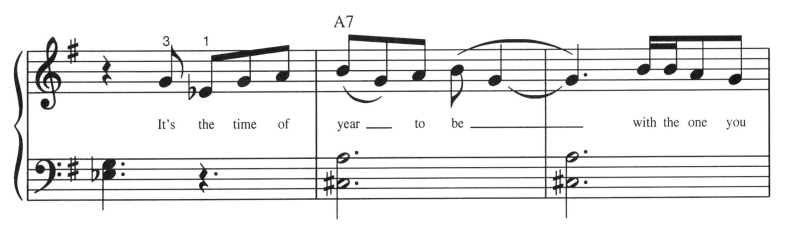

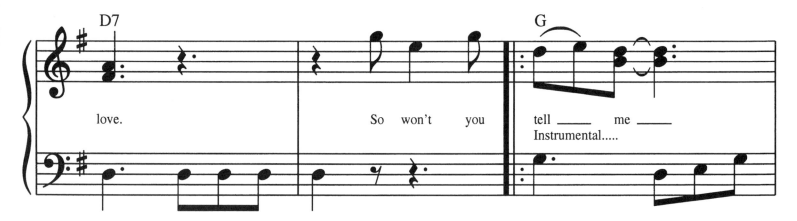

love.

So won't you tell ___ me ___

Instrumental.....

you'll nev - er more ___ roam. ___

Christ - mas and

New Year ___

will find you home.

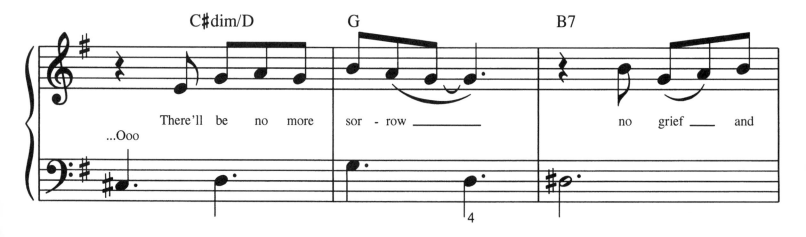

There'll be no more sor - row ___

no grief ___ and

...Ooo

pain _____ and I'll be hap - py _____ hap -

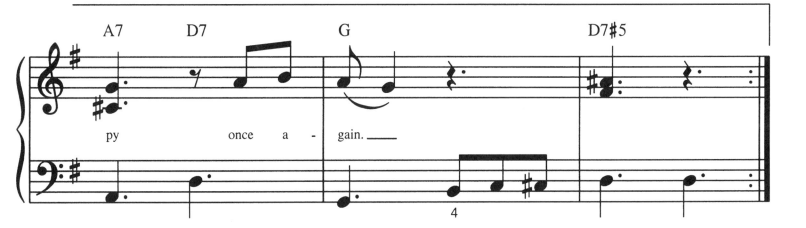

py once a - gain. _____

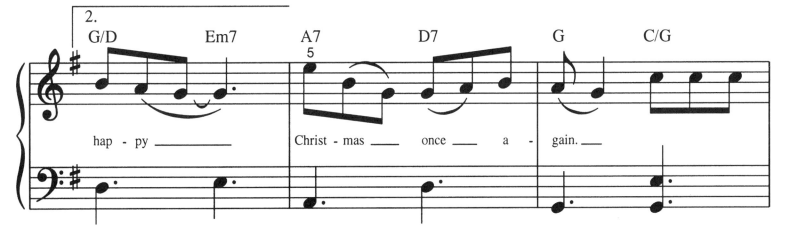

hap - py _____ Christ - mas _____ once _____ a - gain. _____

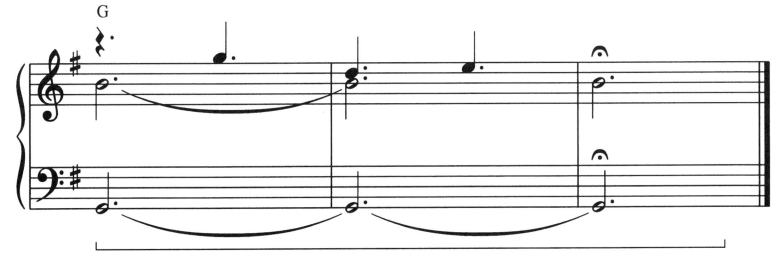

PRETTY PAPER

Words and Music by
WILLIE NELSON

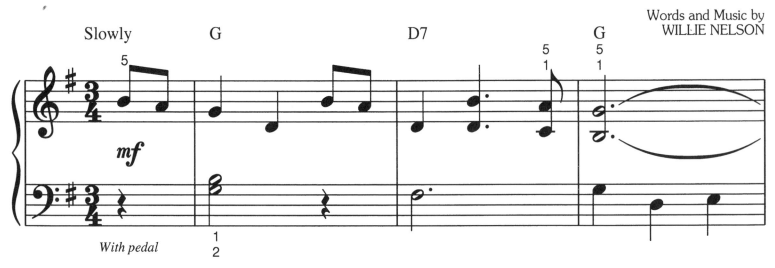

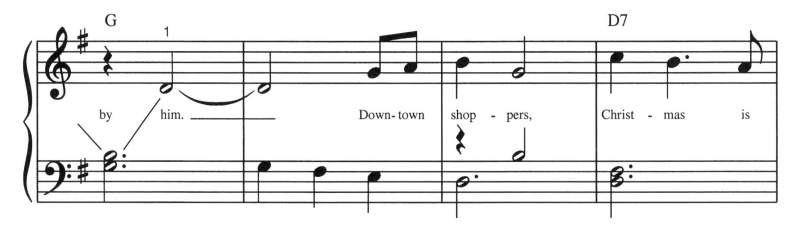

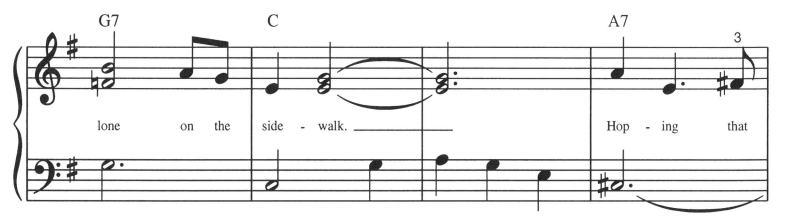

lone on the side - walk. _____ Hop - ing that

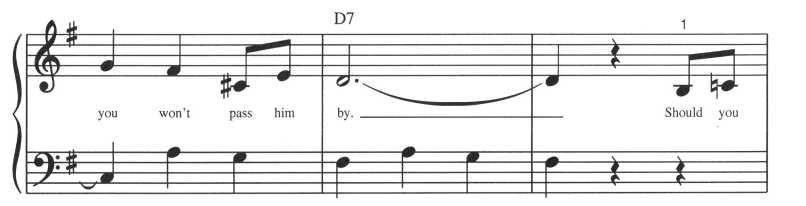

you won't pass him by. _____ Should you

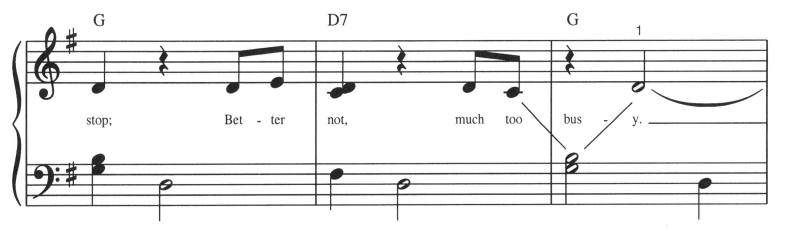

stop; Bet - ter not, much too bus - y. _____

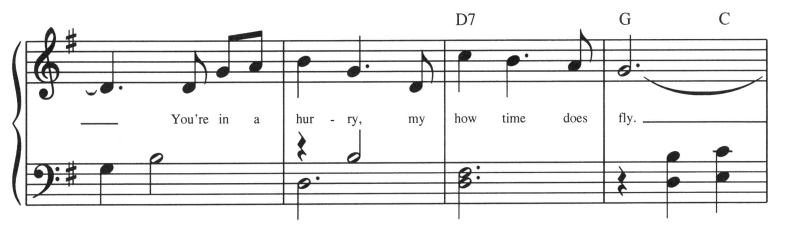

_____ You're in a hur - ry, my how time does fly. _____

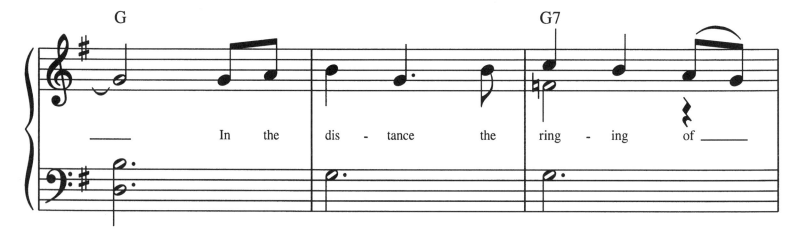

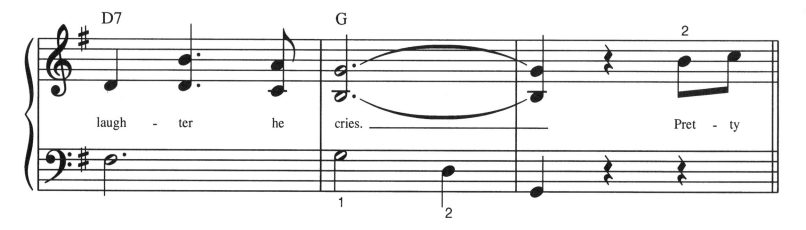

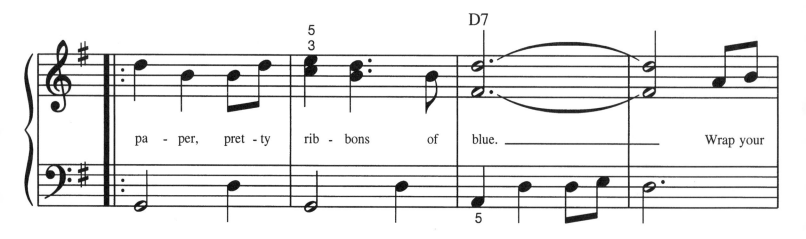

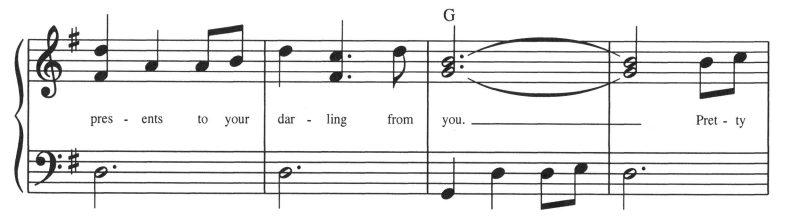

pres - ents   to   your   dar - ling   from   you. _____   Pret - ty

G7   C

pen - cils   to   write,   "I   love   you." _____

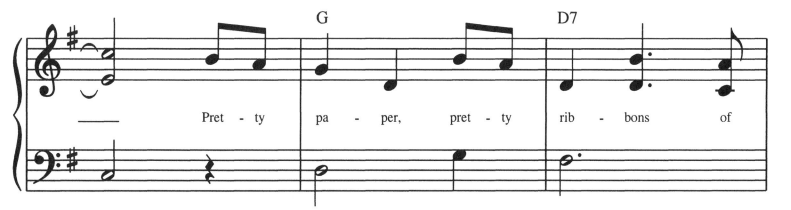

G   D7

_____   Pret - ty   pa - per,   pret - ty   rib - bons   of

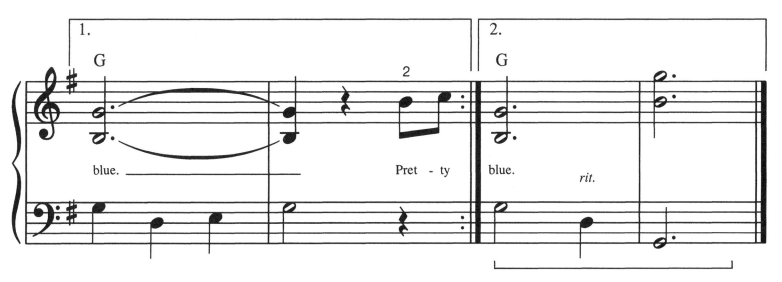

1.   G

blue. _____   Pret - ty

2.   G

blue.   *rit.*

ROCKIN' AROUND THE CHRISTMAS TREE

Music and Lyrics by
JOHNNY MARKS

With a beat

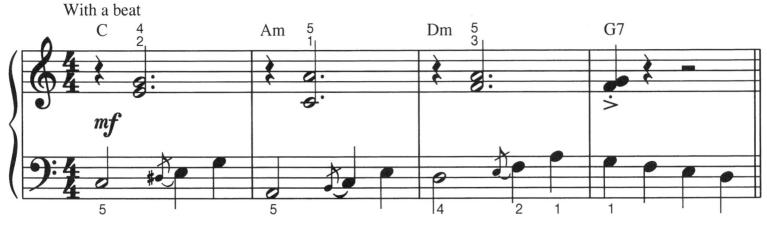

Rock-in' a -round the Christ-mas tree at the Christ-mas par-ty

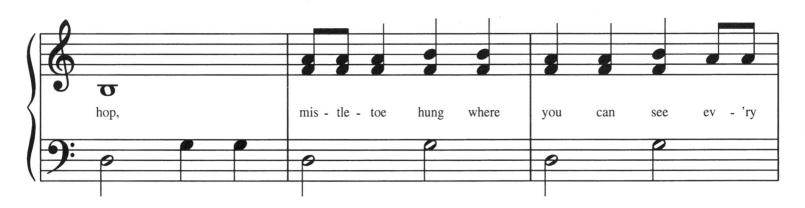

hop, mis-tle-toe hung where you can see ev-'ry

cou-ple tries to stop. Rock-in' a -round the Christ-mas tree, let the

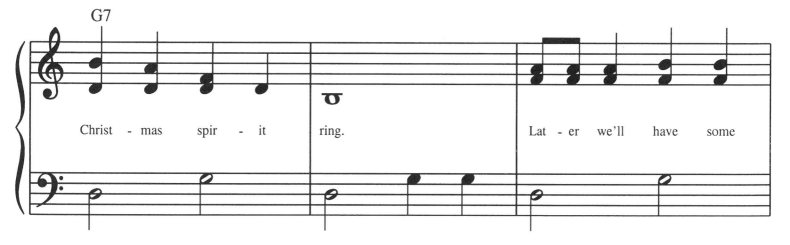

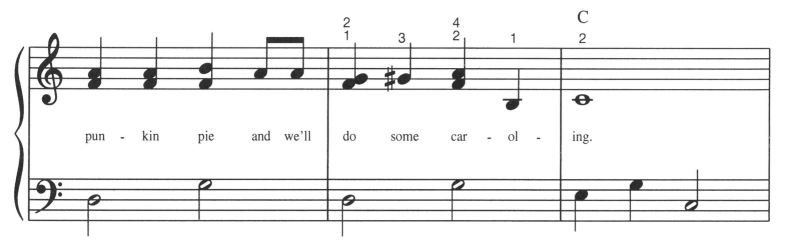

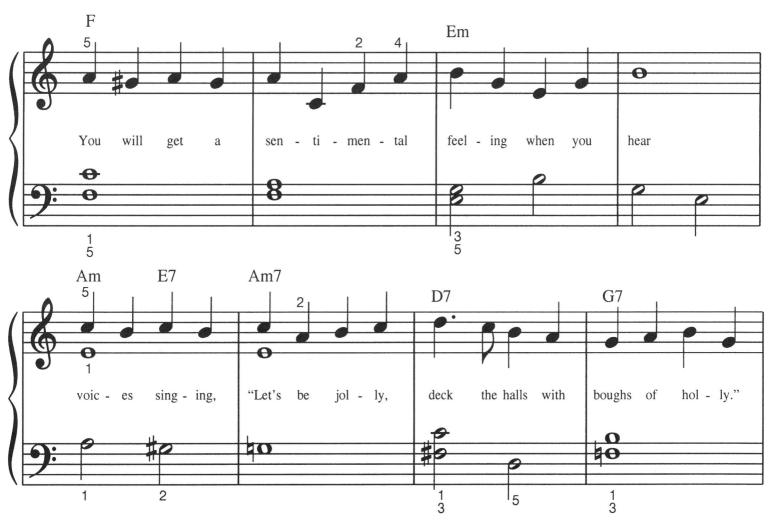

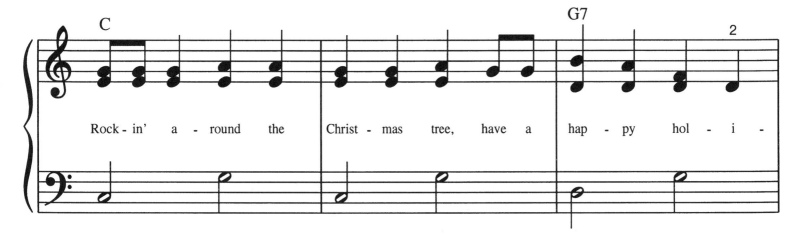

Rock - in' a - round the Christ - mas tree, have a hap - py hol - i -

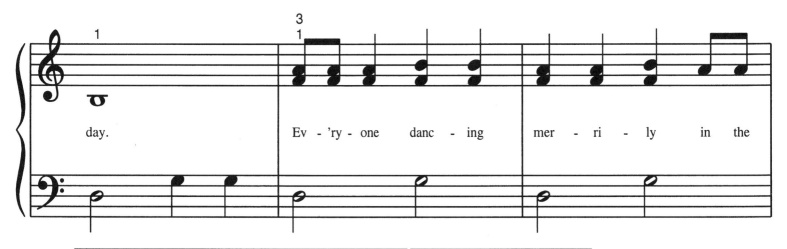

day. Ev - 'ry - one danc - ing mer - ri - ly in the

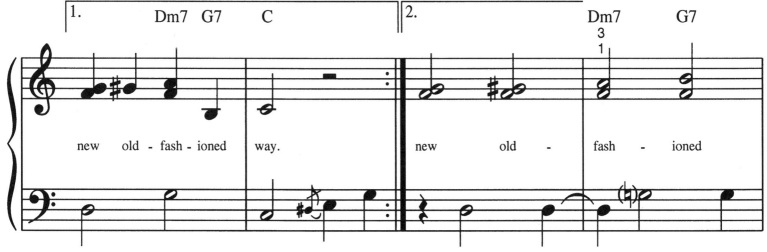

1. Dm7 G7 C 2. Dm7 G7

new old - fash - ioned way. new old - fash - ioned

C

way.

RUDOLPH THE RED-NOSED REINDEER

Music and Lyrics by
JOHNNY MARKS

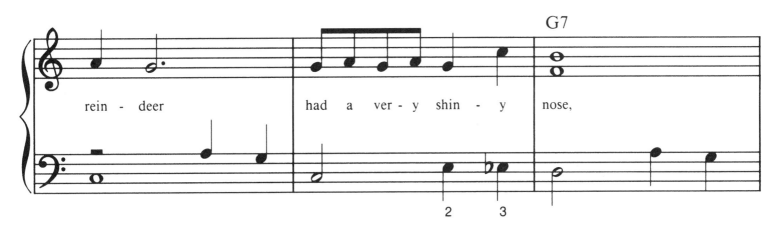

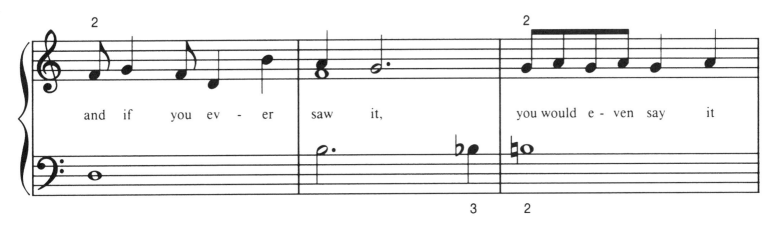

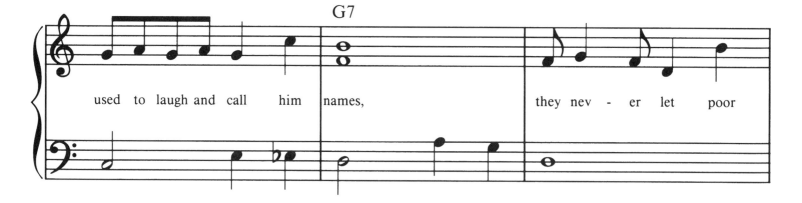

used to laugh and call him names,   they nev - er let poor

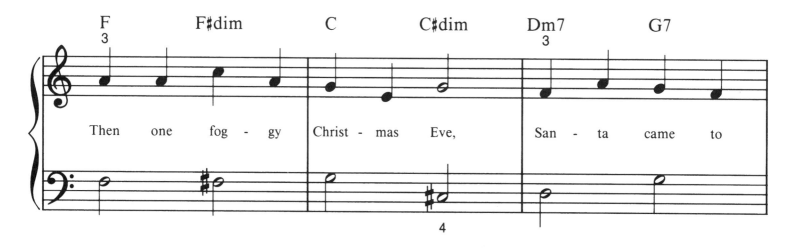

Ru - dolph   join in an - y rein - deer games.

Then one fog - gy   Christ - mas Eve,   San - ta came to

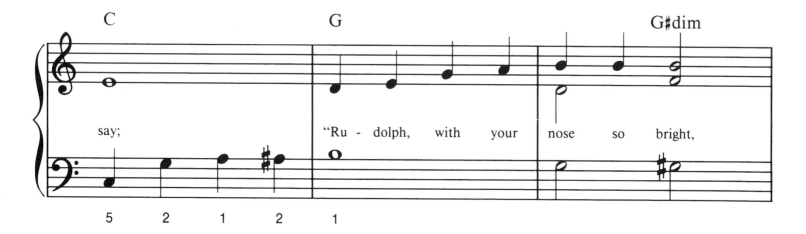

say;   "Ru - dolph, with your   nose so bright,

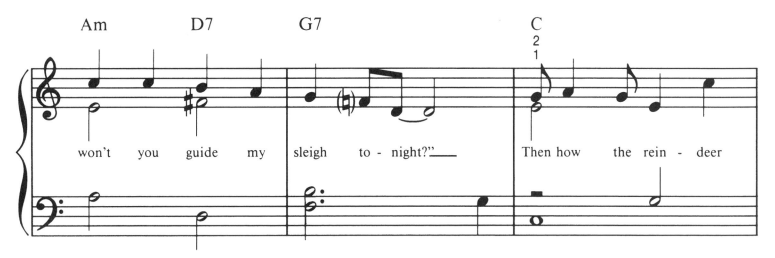

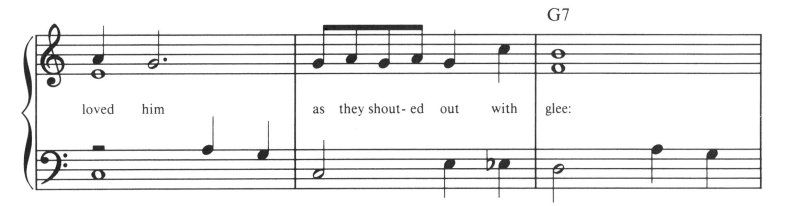

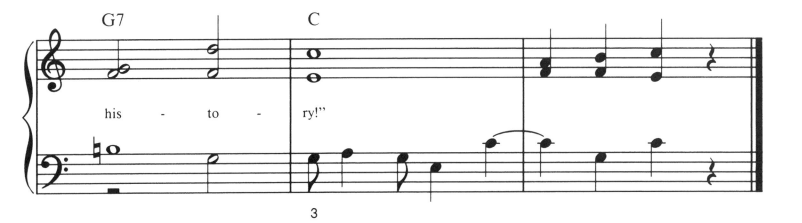

ROCKING

Traditional Czech Carol

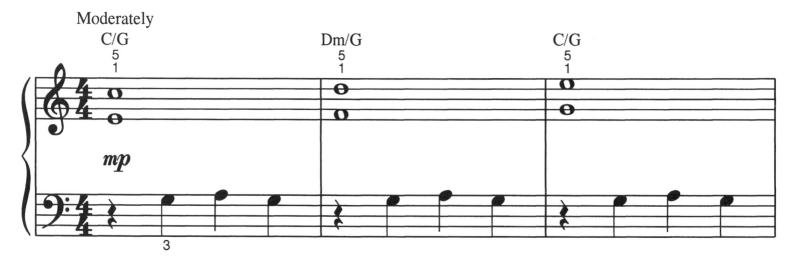

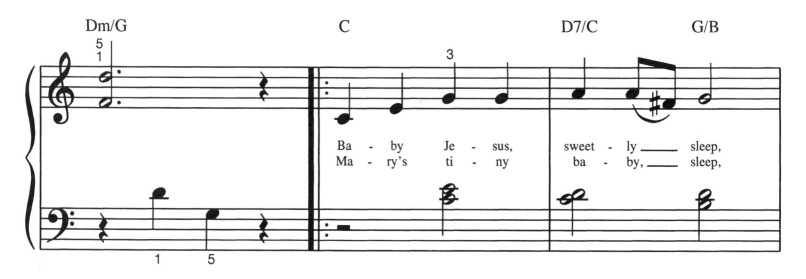

Ba - by Je - sus, sweet - ly _____ sleep,
Ma - ry's ti - ny ba - by, _____ sleep,

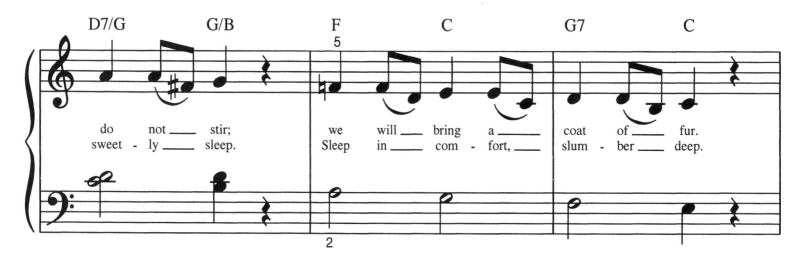

do not _____ stir; we will _____ bring a _____ coat of _____ fur.
sweet - ly _____ sleep. Sleep in _____ com - fort, _____ slum - ber _____ deep.

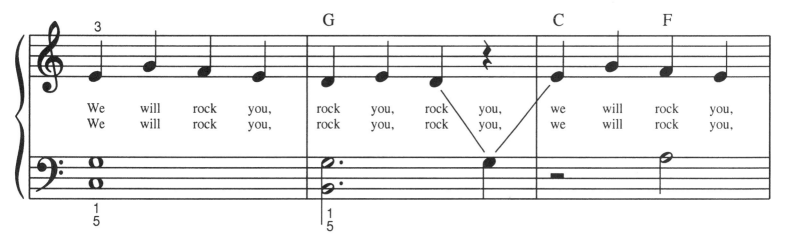

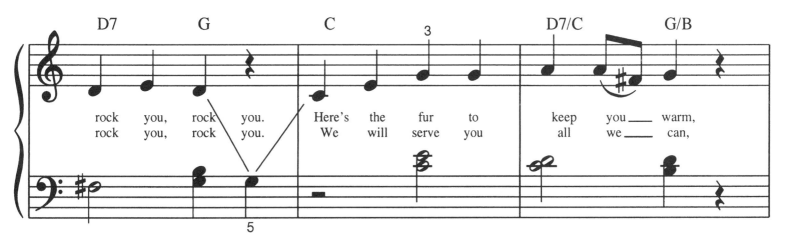

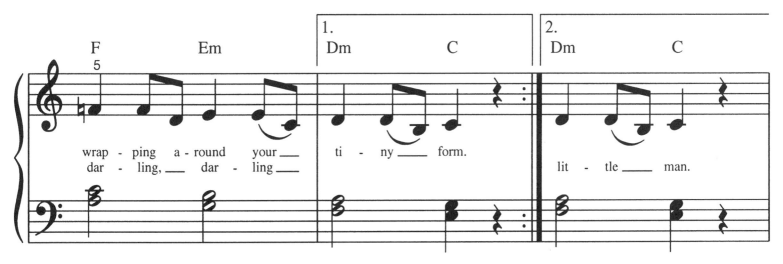

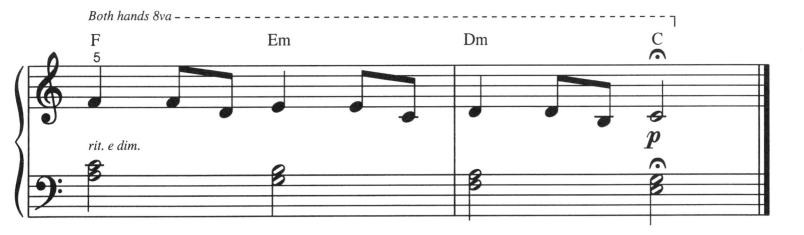

SILENT NIGHT

Words by JOSEPH MOHR
Music by FRANZ GRUBER

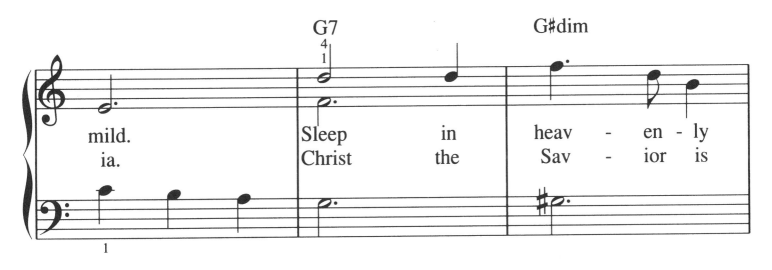

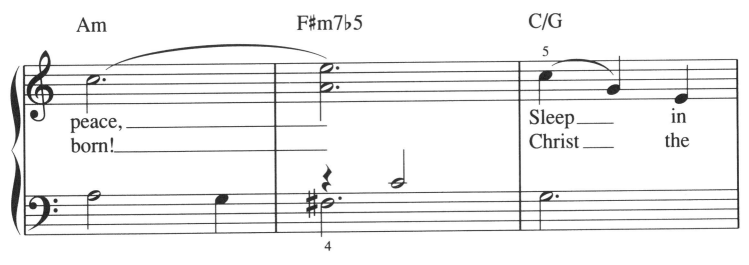

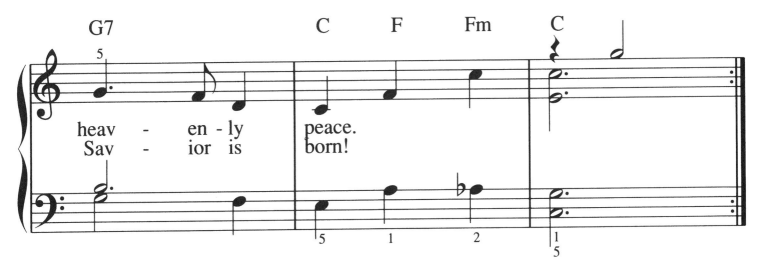

SILVER BELLS

Words and Music by JAY LIVINGSTON
and RAY EVANS

Moderately

with pedal

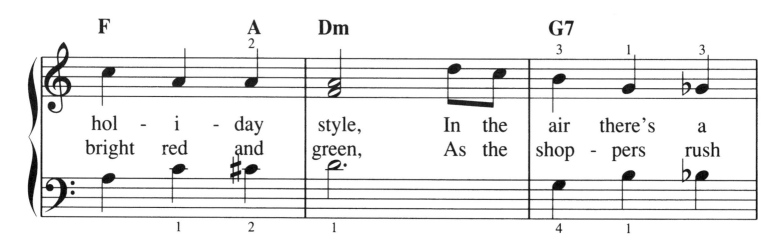

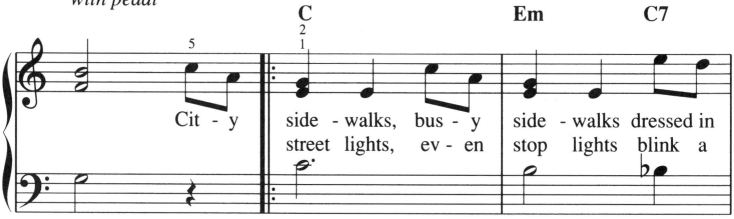

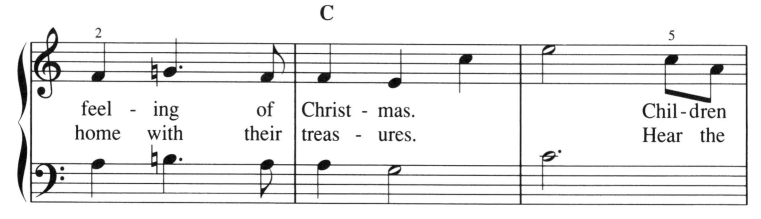

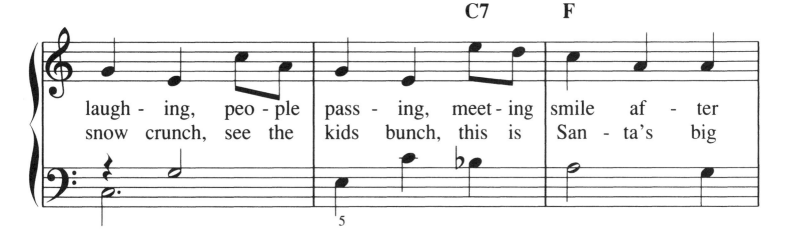

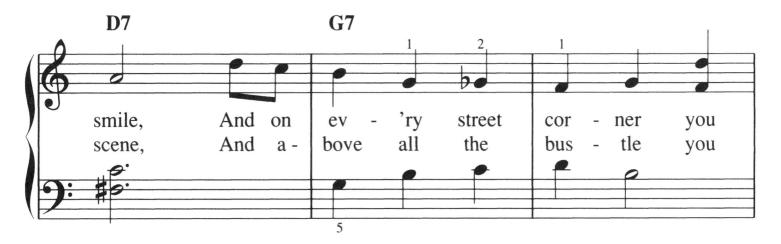

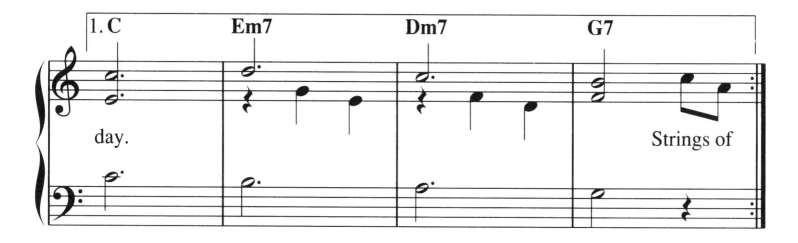

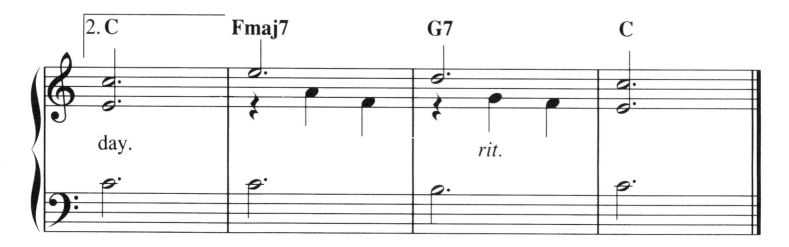

SUZY SNOWFLAKE

Words and Music by SID TEPPER
and ROY BENNETT

Moderately

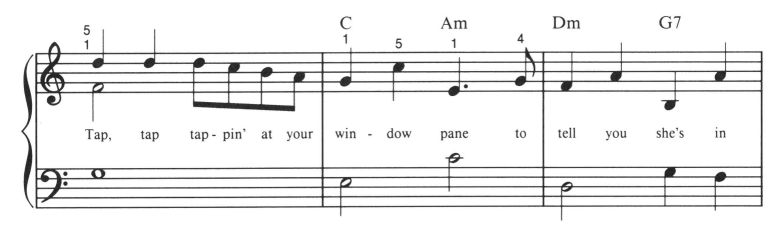

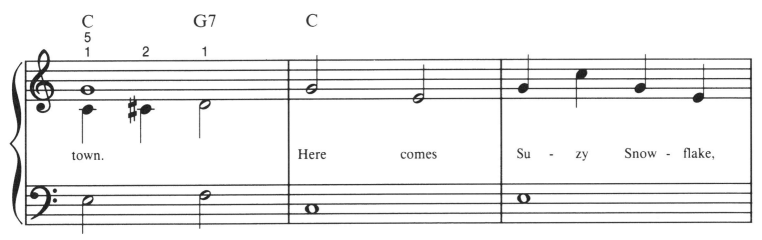

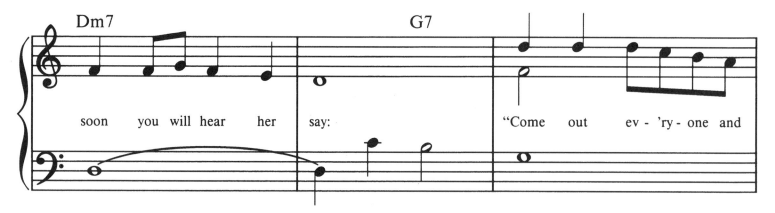

soon you will hear her say: "Come out ev-'ry-one and

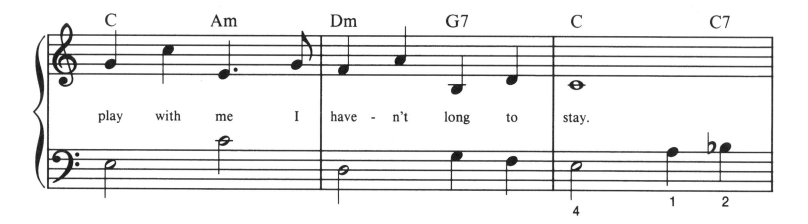

play with me I have-n't long to stay.

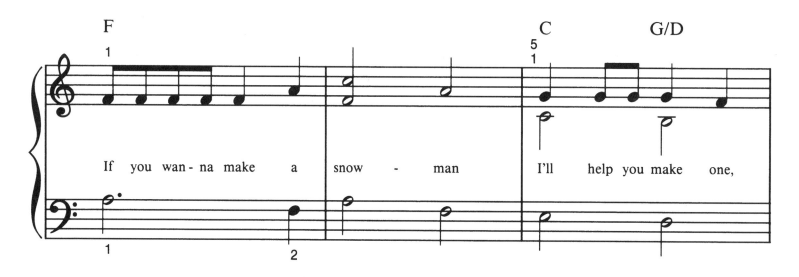

If you wan-na make a snow - man I'll help you make one,

one, two, three. If you wan-na take a sleigh ride,

The ride's on me." Here comes

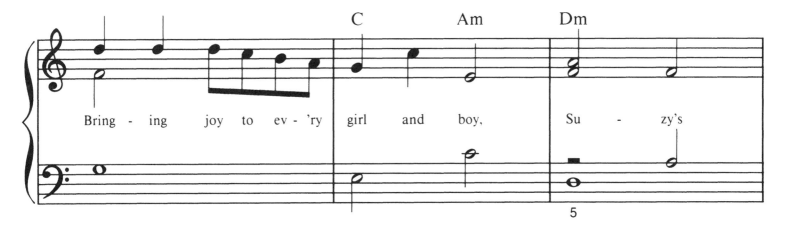

Su - zy Snow - flake, look at her tum - blin' down,

Bring - ing joy to ev - 'ry girl and boy, Su - zy's

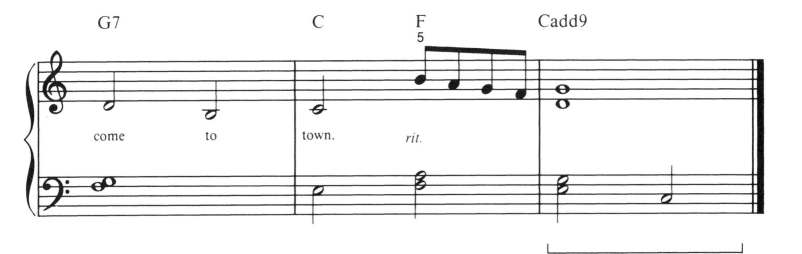

come to town. *rit.*

SUSSEX CAROL

Traditional English Carol

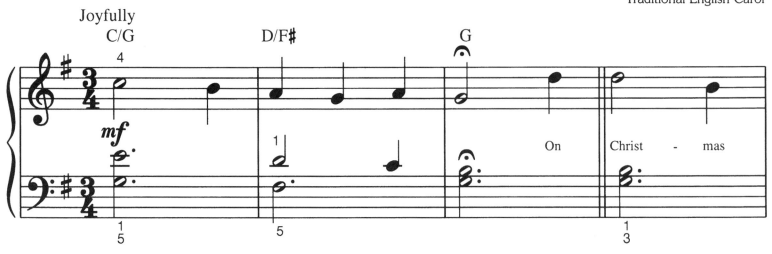

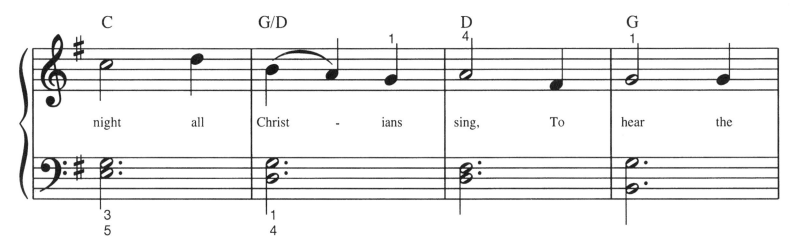

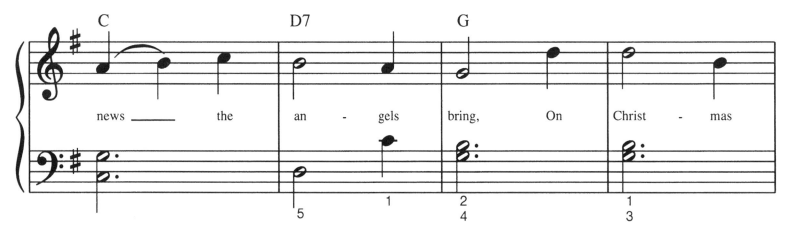

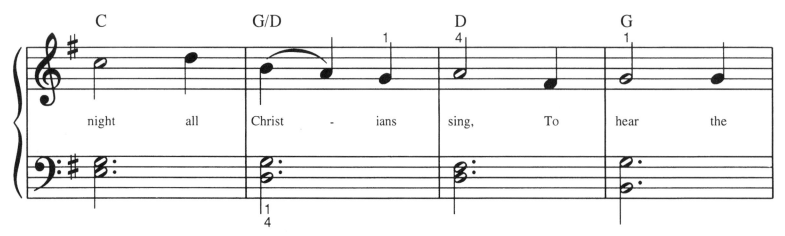

151

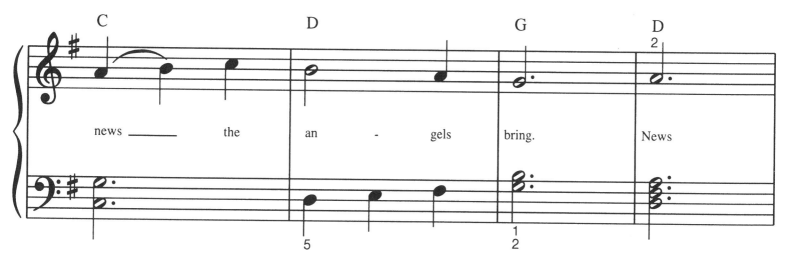

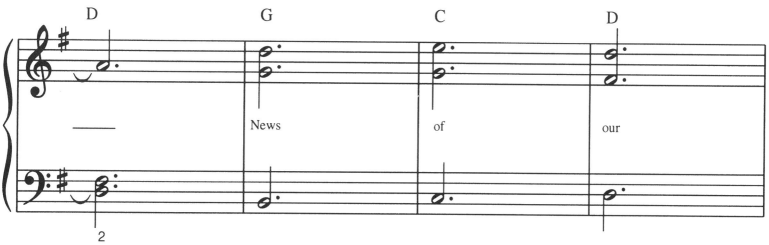

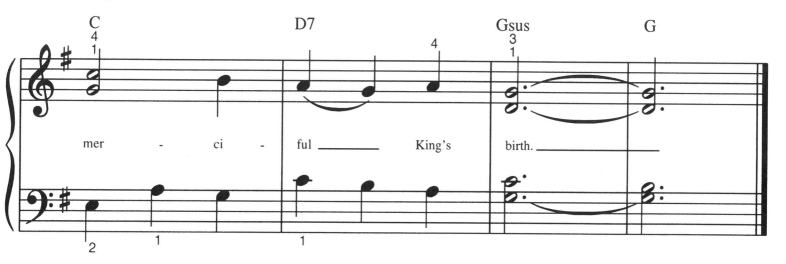

UP ON THE HOUSETOP

Words and Music by
B.R. HANDY

Brightly

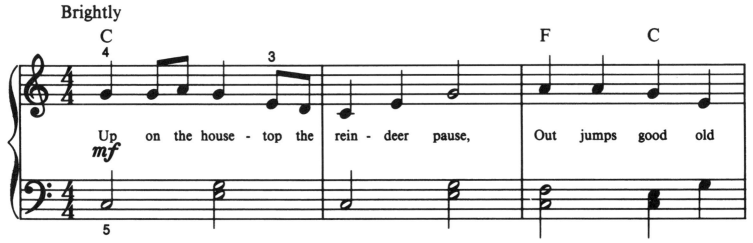

Up on the house-top the rein-deer pause, Out jumps good old

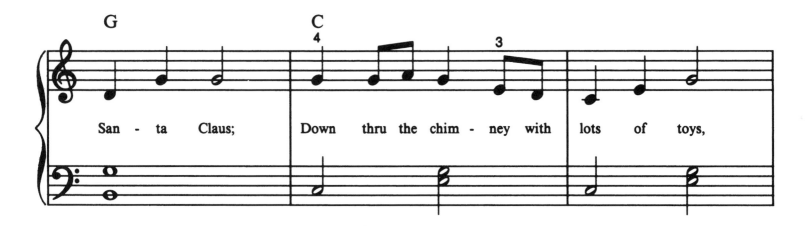

San - ta Claus; Down thru the chim - ney with lots of toys,

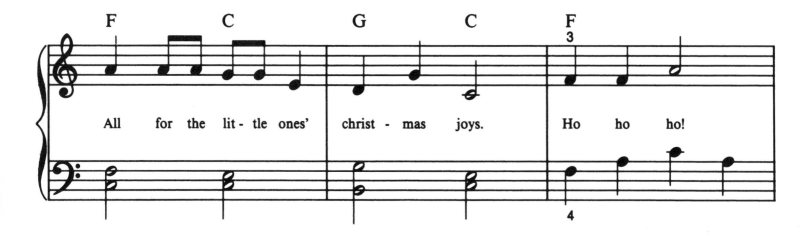

All for the lit - tle ones' christ - mas joys. Ho ho ho!

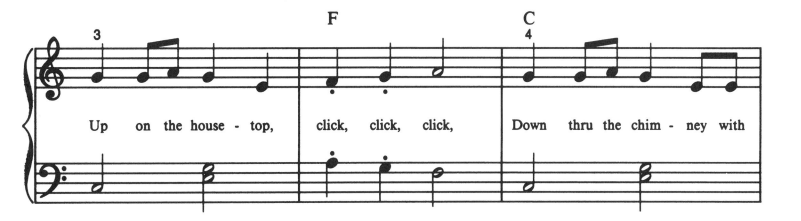

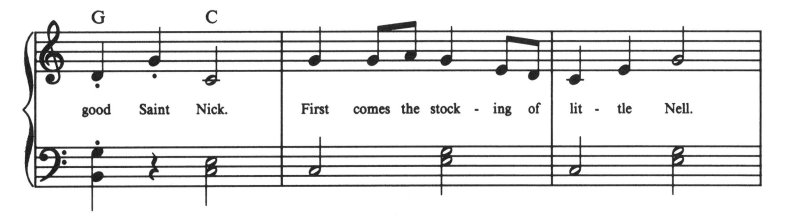

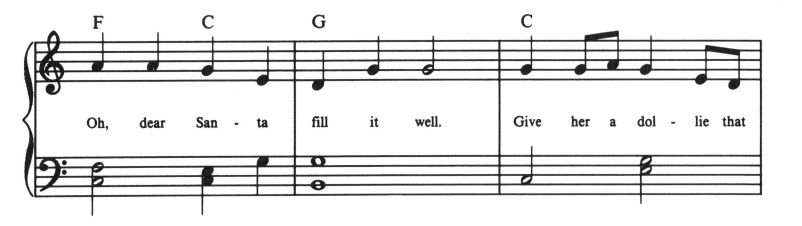

laughs and cries,   One that will o - pen and   shut her eyes.

Ho ho ho!   Who would-n't go!   Ho ho ho!

4

Who would-n't go ——   Up on the house top,   click, click, click.

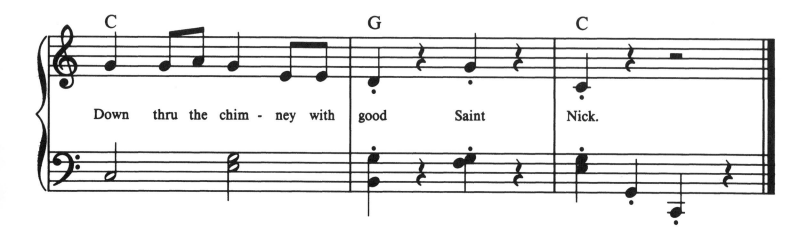

Down thru the chim - ney with   good Saint   Nick.

WE NEED A LITTLE CHRISTMAS
from MAME

Music and Lyric by
JERRY HERMAN

Brightly, in 2 (𝅗𝅥 = 1 beat)

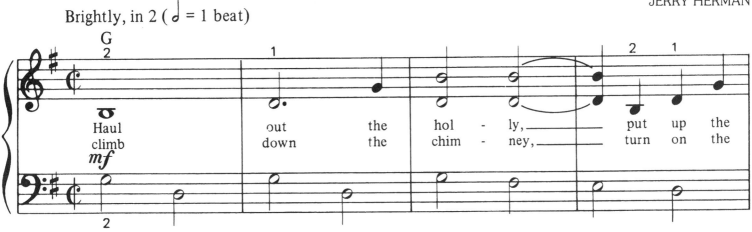

Haul out the hol - ly,___ put up the
climb down the chim - ney,___ turn on the

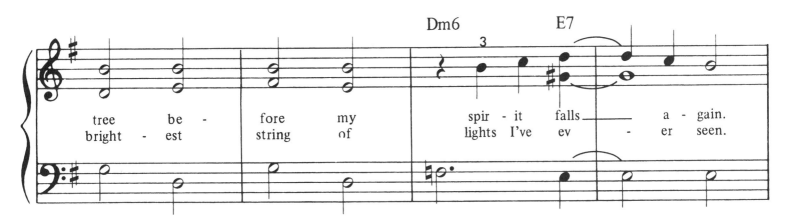

tree be - fore my spir - it falls___ a - gain.
bright - est string of lights I've ev - er seen.

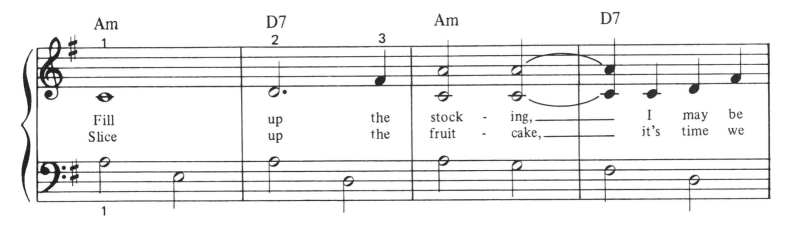

Fill up the stock - ing,___ I may be
Slice up the fruit - cake,___ it's time we

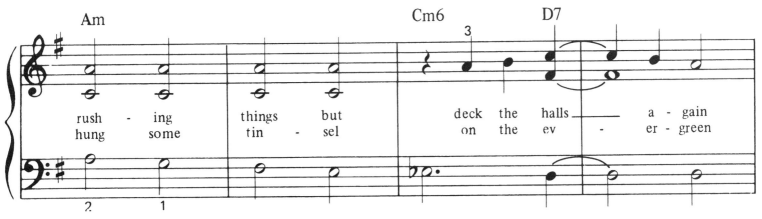

rush - ing things but deck the halls___ a - gain
hung some things tin - sel on the ev - er - green

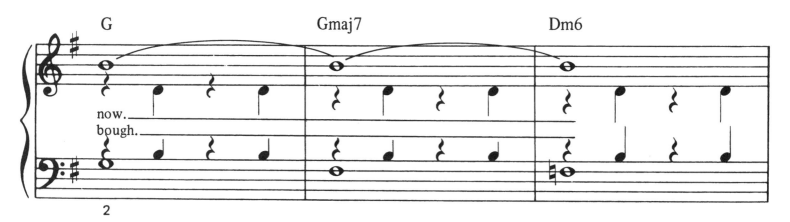

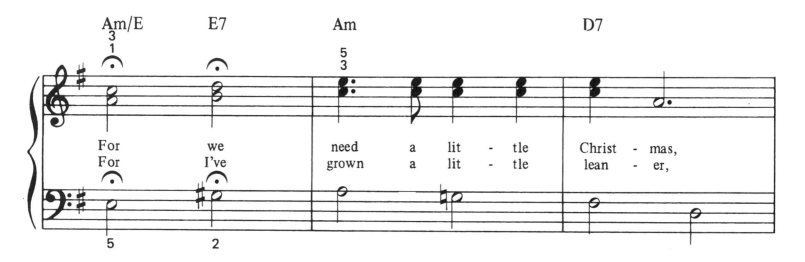

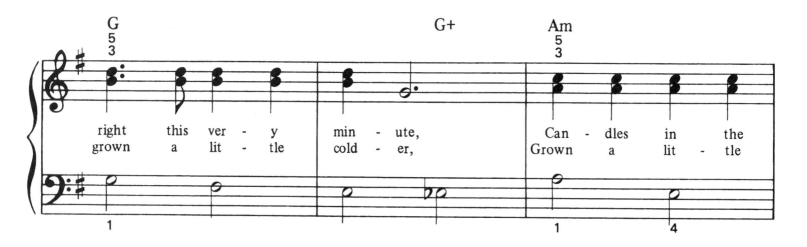

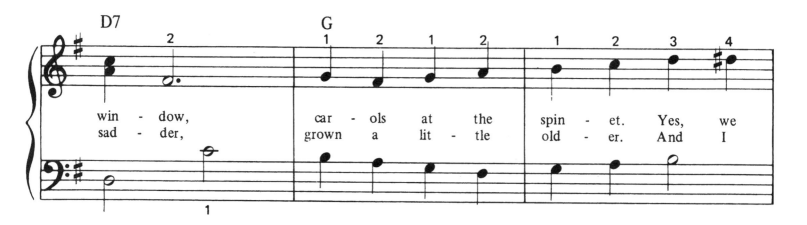

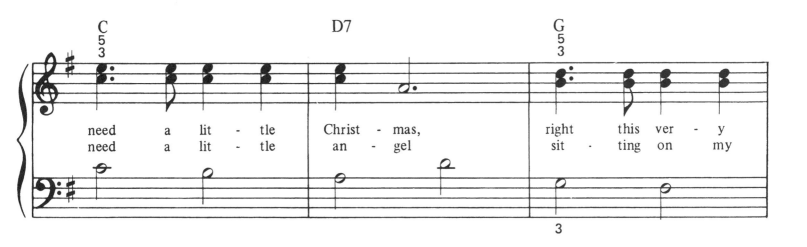

need a lit - tle
need a lit - tle

Christ - mas,
an - gel

right this ver - y
sit - ting on my

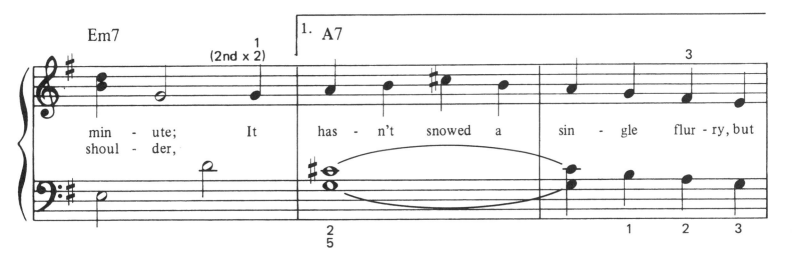

min - ute; It
shoul - der,

has - n't snowed a

sin - gle flur - ry, but

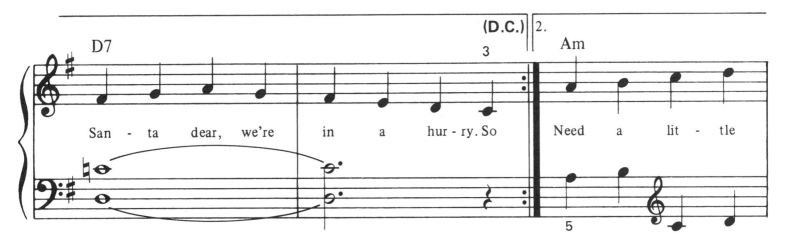

San - ta dear, we're

in a hur - ry. So

Need a lit - tle

Christ - mas

now!

WE THREE KINGS OF ORIENT ARE

Words and Music by
JOHN H. HOPKINS

Gently and quietly

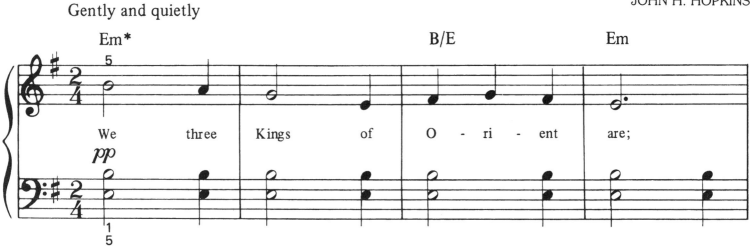

We three Kings of O - ri - ent are;

pp

Bear - ing gifts we tra - verse a - far,

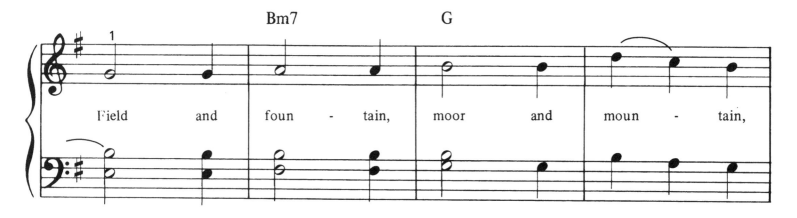

Field and foun - tain, moor and moun - tain,

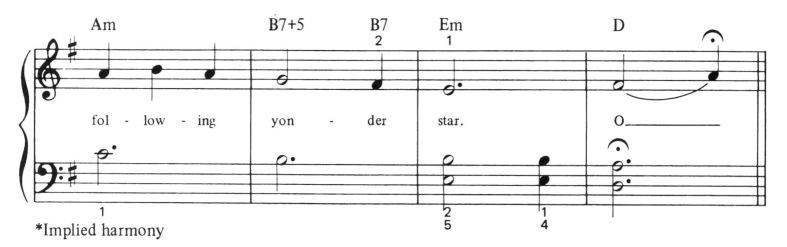

fol - low - ing yon - der star. O_____

*Implied harmony

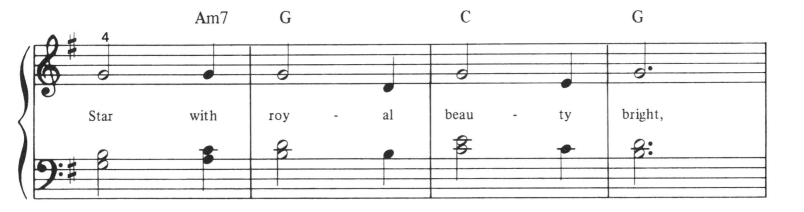

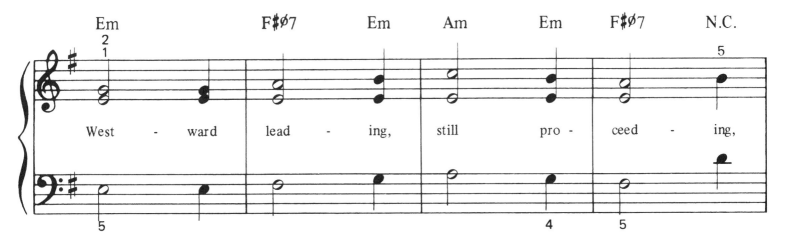

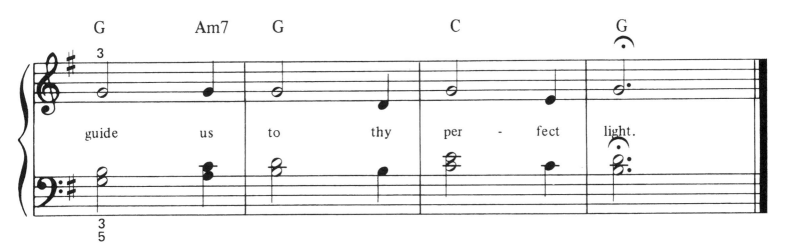

WE WISH YOU A MERRY CHRISTMAS

Traditional English Folksong

Brightly

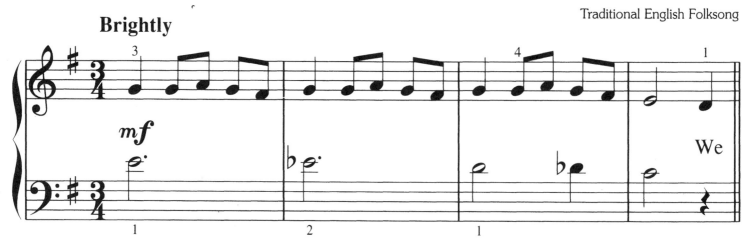

We

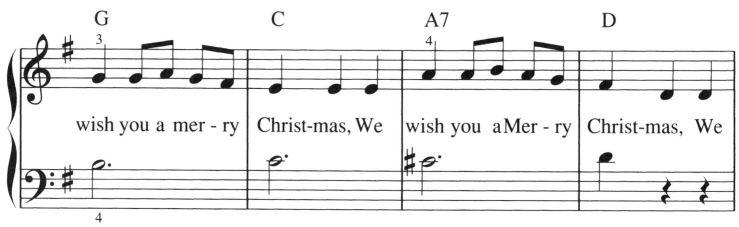

wish you a mer - ry Christ-mas, We wish you a Mer - ry Christ-mas, We

wish you a Mer - ry Christ-mas and a hap - py New Year. Good

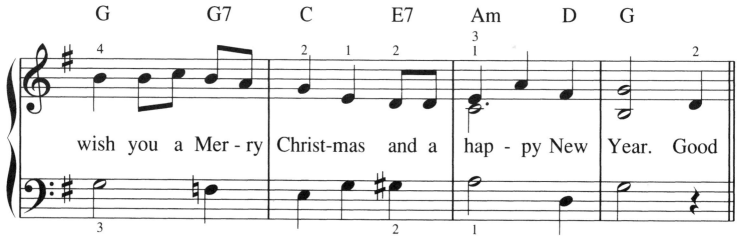

ti - dings we bring to you and your kin, Good

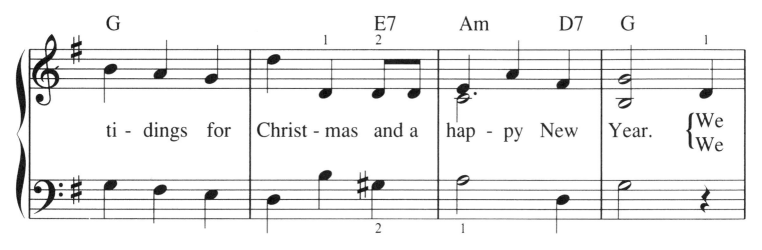

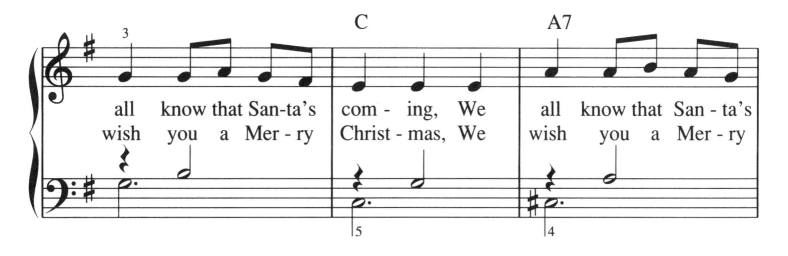

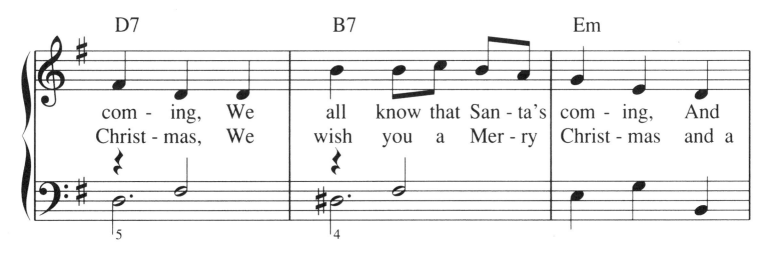

WHAT CHILD IS THIS?

Words by WILLIAM C. DIX
16th Century English Melody

Gently, not too slow

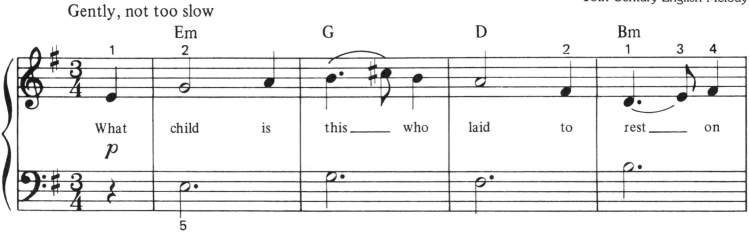

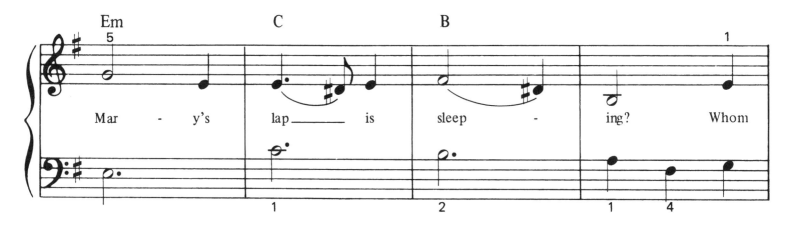

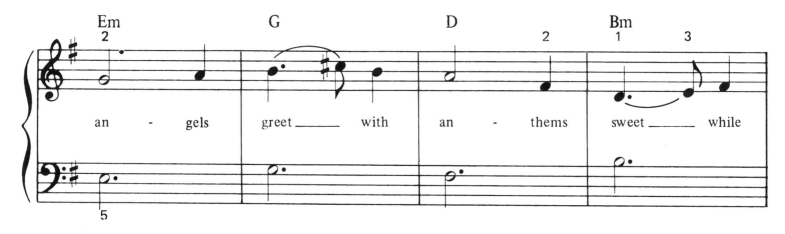

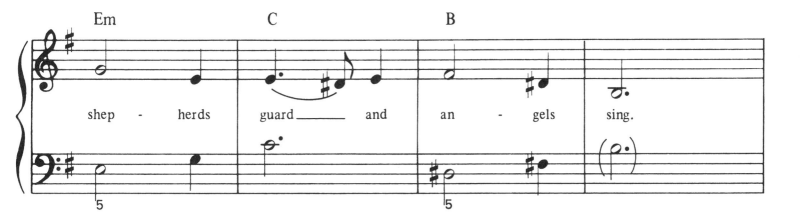

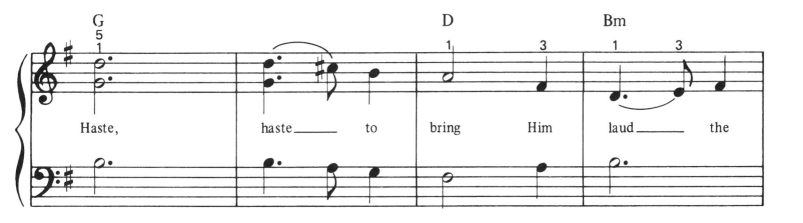

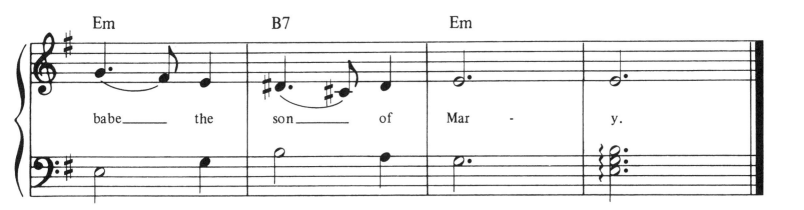

WONDERFUL CHRISTMASTIME

Words and Music by
McCARTNEY

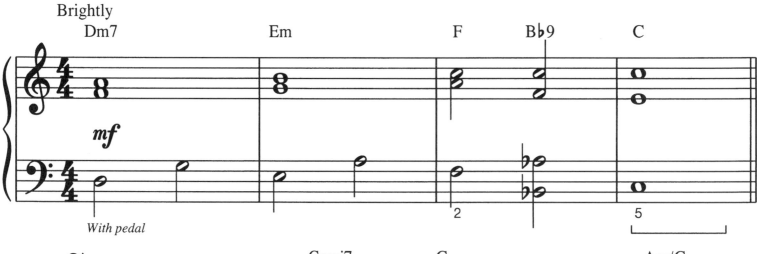

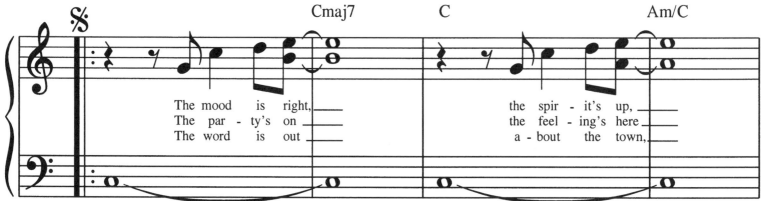

The mood is right, _____ the spir - it's up, _____
The par - ty's on _____ the feel - ing's here _____
The word is out _____ a - bout the town, _____

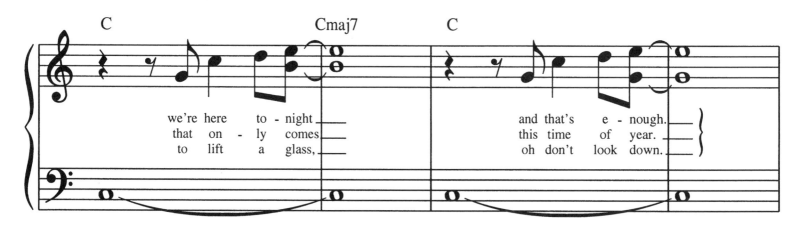

we're here to - night _____ and that's e - nough. _____
that on - ly comes _____ this time of year. _____
to lift a glass, _____ oh don't look down. _____

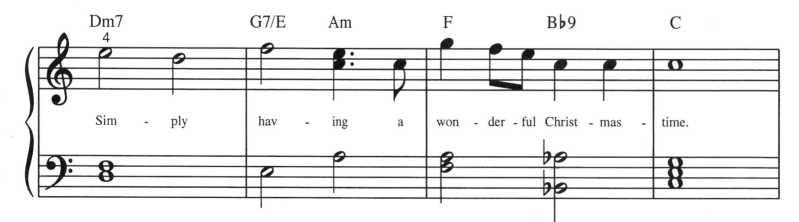

Sim - ply hav - ing a won - der - ful Christ - mas - time.

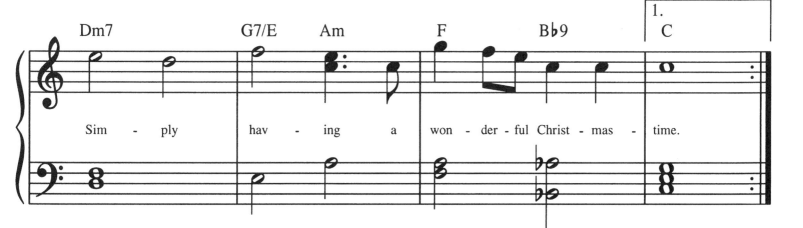

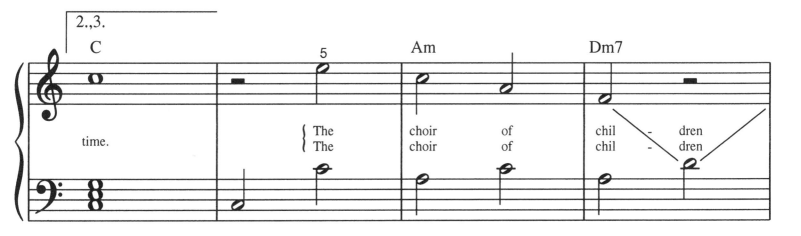

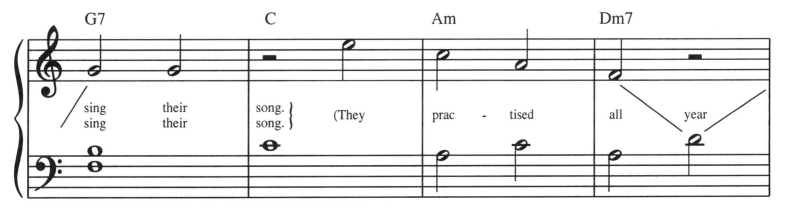

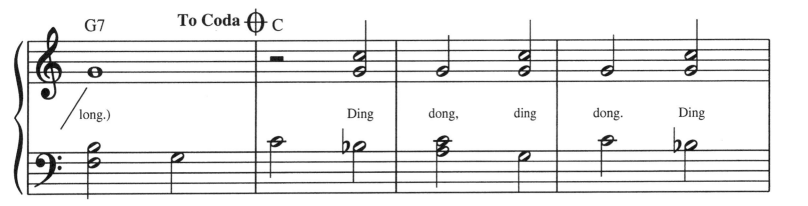

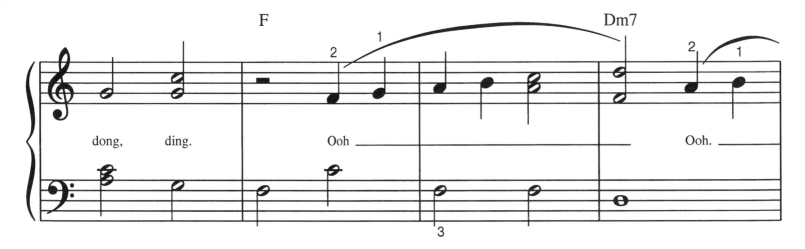

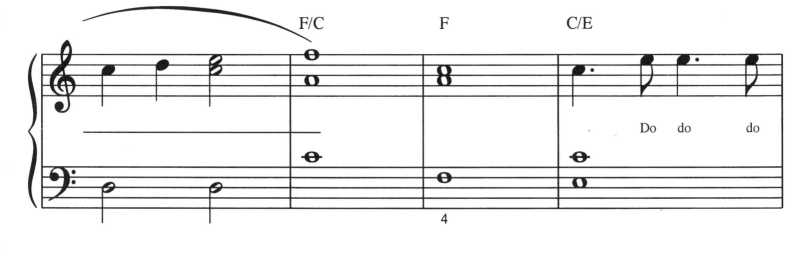

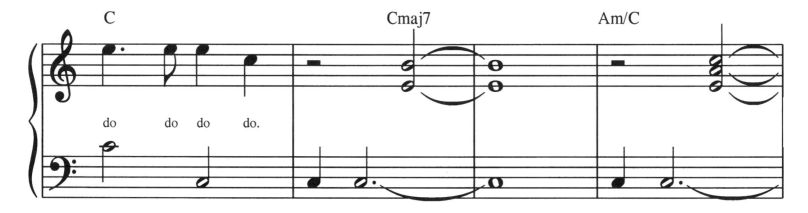

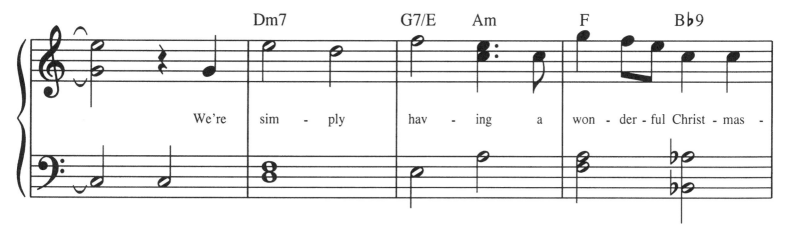

We're sim - ply hav - ing a won - der - ful Christ - mas -

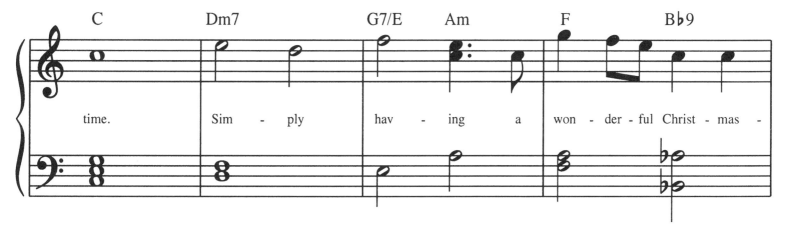

time. Sim - ply hav - ing a won - der - ful Christ - mas -

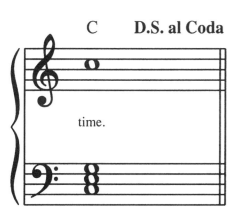

time.

D.S. al Coda

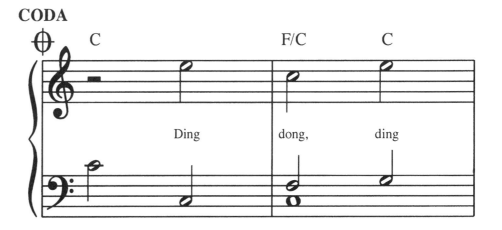

CODA

Ding dong, ding

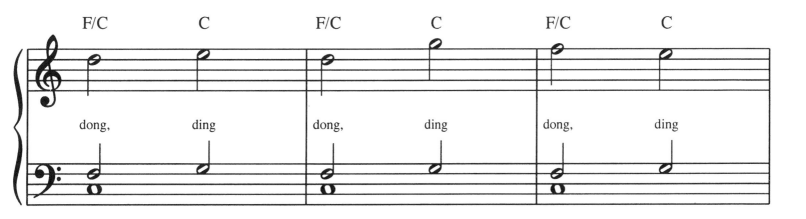

dong, ding dong, ding dong, ding

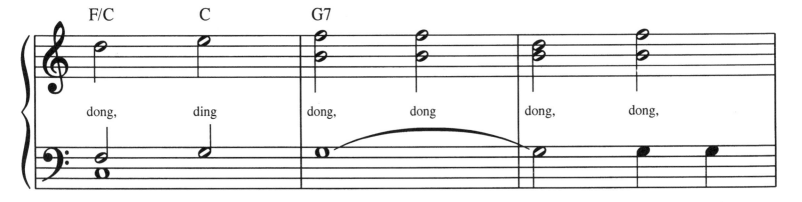

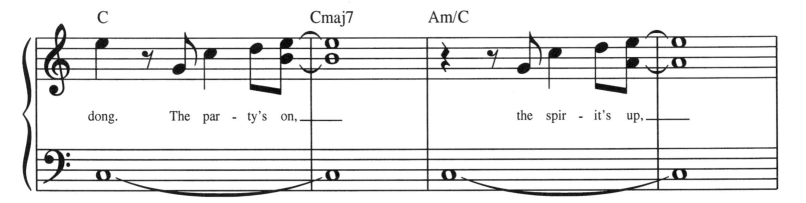

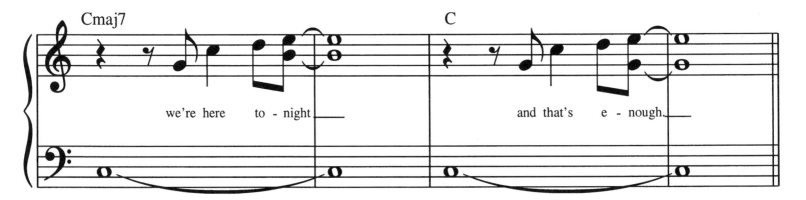

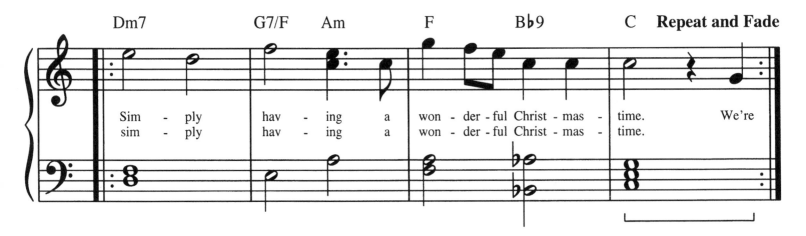